CHARTING THE STOCK MARKET

THE WYCKOFF METHOD

CHARTING THE STOCK MARKET

THE WYCKOFF METHOD

Edited by

Jack K. Hutson

Technical Analysis, Inc.

Seattle, Washington • U.S.A.

http://www.**Traders**.com

SAN 661-5317 Technical Analysis, Inc., Seattle, WA 98116-4499

Library of Congress Cataloging in Publication Data

Hutson, Jack K., 1948-
Charting the Stock Market: The Wyckoff Method /
Jack K. Hutson
p. cm.
Includes bibliographies and indices.
ISBN 0-938773-06-2

Contents: 1. Hutson, Jack K. 2. Title: Charting the Stock Market: The Wyckoff Method. 3. Title: Stocks & Commodities. 4. Technical Analysis, Inc. I. Title.

Library of Congress catalog card number: 91-66714

10 9 8 7 6 5 4 3 2

Contents

Preface

The contents of this book are derived from the pages of *Technical Analysis of* STOCKS & COMMODITIES, a magazine that documents and explains practical trading techniques for stocks, bonds, mutual funds, options and commodities.

The contributors included in this book are longtime students of the Wyckoff Method. Craig F. Schroeder is educational director of Stock Market Institute Inc. and writes daily commentary from a Wyckoff point of view. David H. Weis publishes the *Technical Forces* newsletter, focusing on market analysis using the methods of R.N. Elliott and Richard D. Wyckoff. And as the publisher of *Technical Analysis of* STOCKS & COMMODITIES magazine, I wrote the series of articles appearing in the first part of this book after having spent several years of research on Wyckoff's writings in an effort to improve my own short-term trading.

The Wyckoff Method, a common-sense approach to trading that emphasizes study, practice, and risk limitation, studies the motion of the market. With this simple goal, the trader can avoid being influenced by all the rumors, information and misinformation that inundates Wall Street everyday and concentrate instead on the direction of the market and the position of a stock or bond in relation to the market. The Wyckoff Method also takes into account investor psychology and provides insight into how and why professional traders buy and sell issues. Without this understanding of the underlying forces in the market, it is impossible for you to compete in a professional's game.

Jack K. Hutson

PART I

Principles of the Wyckoff Method

by Jack K. Hutson

1
The Early Days

Anyone who buys or sells a stock, a bond, or a commodity for profit is speculating if he employs intelligent foresight. If he does not, he is gambling.

— Richard D. Wyckoff, American pioneer in technical stock analysis.

Richard Wyckoff's first instruction to students of his stock analysis method published in the 1930s was quite simple and specific — forget all the decision-making factors you ever used. All you need to know can be found in the tables of stock prices and volumes in your daily newspaper.

With this back-to-basics approach, Wyckoff promised to show his students "the real rules of the game" played so adroitly by well-heeled investors with enough capital to pack clout in the market.

Although it's hard to imagine anything remaining viable from the 1930s to the 1990s, especially a stock market technique, the Richard D. Wyckoff method of trading and investing stocks has survived the times as a classic. Whatever it lacks in glamour and gee-whiz in this computerized age, it makes up by giving its users a solid foundation for analyzing the fundamental relationships among the market's primary forces. In this respect, it's like the classic (and time-honored) point and figure chart. It can be improved but not outdated.

Take a look at Wyckoff's goals — to select only stocks that will move soonest, fastest and farthest in bear or bull markets; to limit losses and let profits run; and to make the most efficient use of investment capital. Hardly an antiquated outlook.

It also is a universal theory. The premises are applicable to any open market — stocks, bonds, options or commodities.

Wyckoff was intrigued by the stock market. He learned the market from the bottom up, at a time when experience was the only teacher. His first job in 1888 was as a 15-year-old stock runner, scurrying back and forth on Wall Street, delivering and exchanging securities and payments for a brokerage firm. By 1898 he had advanced to auditor of another brokerage firm and made his first $1,000 profit in the stock market selling 300 shares of a company with a new product — a pneumatic horse collar. At the age of 25, he opened his own brokerage office.

He had seen "appalling losses in securities suffered annually by millions of people who do not realize what they are risking and have an amazingly small knowledge of the market." He sent daily letters on market conditions to his clients and turned his research and writing into a monthly magazine in 1907.

As a broker, he saw the behind-the-scenes plays of the large operators and realized "it was possible to judge the future course of the market by its own action...that the action of stocks reflected the plans and purposes of those who dominated them...that the basic law of supply and demand governed all price changes; that the best indicator of the future course of the market was the relation of supply to demand."

He published the first technical analysis method of its kind in 1908 and, at the insistence of his readers, began publishing weekly forecasts in 1911, employing charts of price and volume movements for his analysis.

Wyckoff disagreed with analysts who used their charts as a kind of Rorschach test, searching for telltale shapes and formations that would signal whether to buy, sell, or hold steady. "Stock market technique is not an exact science," he would tell his students. "Stock prices are made by the minds of men." In his estimation, mechanical or purely mathematical chart analyses could not compete with finely honed and practiced judgment.

Wyckoff also shunned brokers' offices, financial reports, news items, earnings reports and especially tips, rumors, and "the half-baked trading theories expounded in boardrooms and popular books on the stock market."

To his way of thinking, an analyst should be a detective uncovering the forces behind price and volume fluctuations, a market psychologist weighing the human motivations that fuel those moves, and a general planning a financial campaign to intercept stocks when the charts show them to be at their most profitable stages.

Wyckoff's popularity as an analyst grew dramatically. Even when he tried to limit the size of his following by nearly doubling the price of his publication, the subscriptions totaled $60,000 in six weeks. By his own account, he "made a great deal of money for myself and my clients and subscribers who numbered in excess of 200,000" before his health began to fail and he completely turned his publications and advisory services over to his associates in 1928.

When his method was published as a correspondence course in 1931, he called it "the cream of what I have learned in 40 years of active experience in Wall Street." His method rests squarely on the law of supply and demand. When demand for a stock exceeds supply, prices rise; when supply is greater than demand, prices

Figure 1.1 *(see next page) Vertical line charts record the high, low, and close for individual stocks, stock groups or composite averages. The volume (number of issues traded) is plotted at the bottom of the chart.*

Figure 1.2 *(see next page) Figure charts (also called point & figure charts) only record price. A minimum price movement by the stock is required to update the chart. The figure chart of Boeing is a one-point chart, so price fluctuations of less than one point are ignored. Time is not a factor in recording price but for recordkeeping the single letter of each month may be recorded.*

FIGURE 1.1

Example of vertical line chart (Boeing)

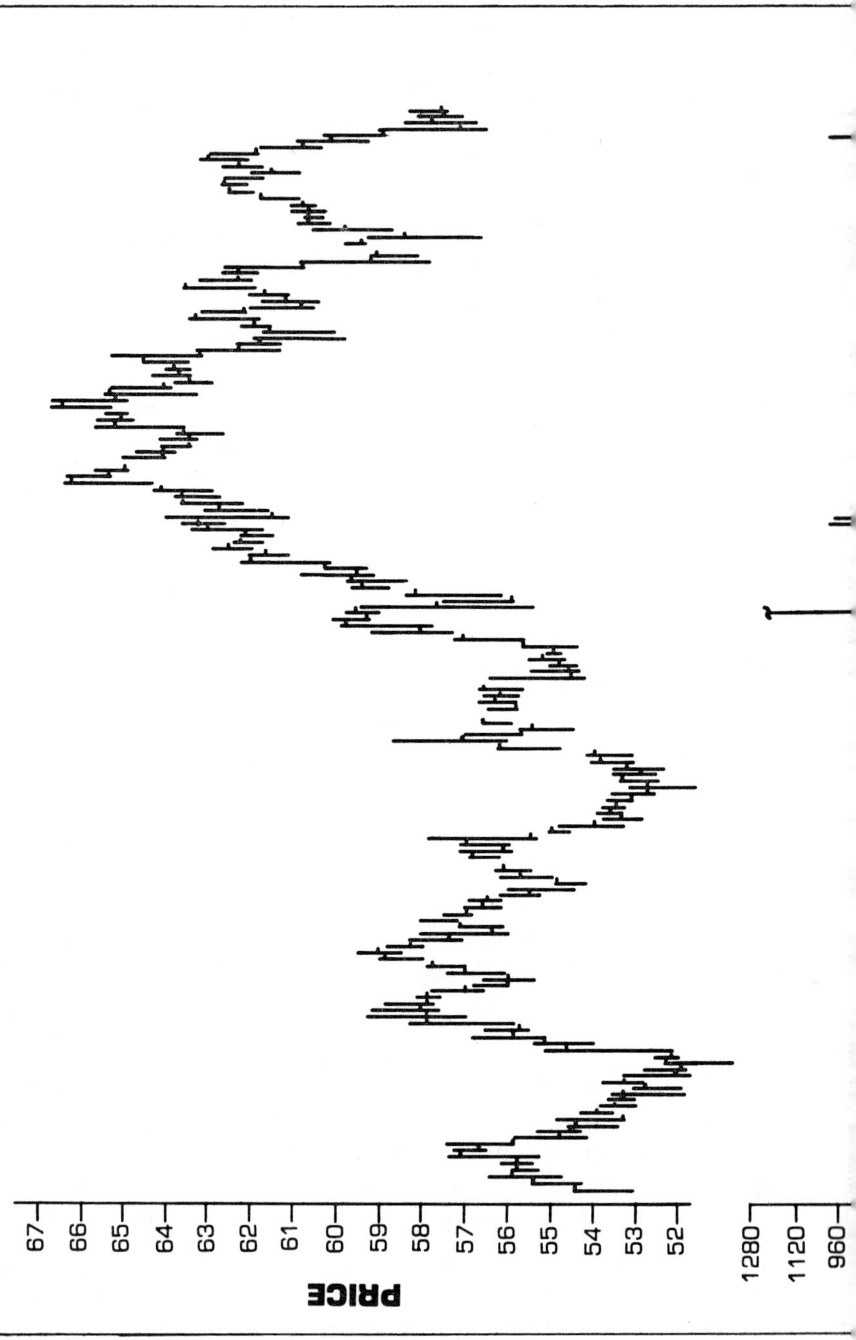

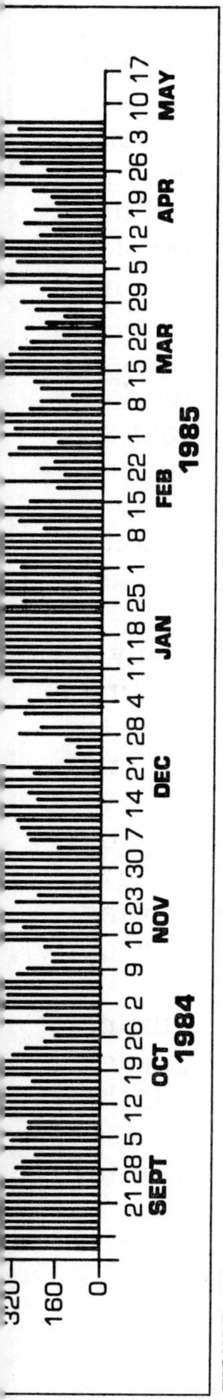

FIGURE 1.2

Example of figure chart (Boeing)

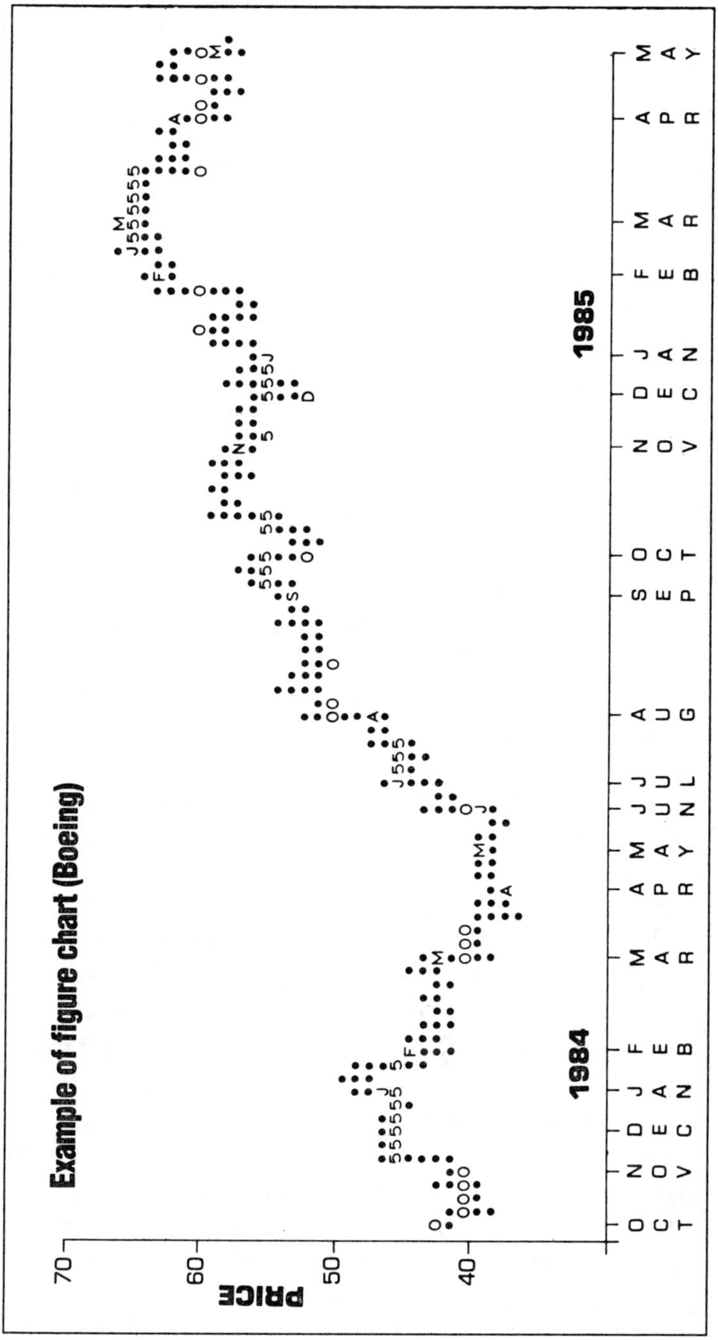

decline. He likens the stock market ticker tape to a movie: "Every minute of the day it is demonstrating whether supply or demand is the greater."

Wyckoff's method charts price, volume and their relationships over time to judge how the market, groups of stocks and individual issues are reacting to the supply-and-demand tug of war. The search is for turning points — the final top of a rising bull market, the final low in a declining bear market and the crests or troughs of the intermediate and minor moves that come in between.

He is guided by the fact that every change in the market consists of waves of buying and selling that last just as long as they can attract a following. When the following is exhausted for the time being, the wave ends and a contrary wave sets in.

Small daily waves build into larger three- to five-point waves, which eventually build into the bull and bear market swings of 10 to 20 points or more.

He acts in harmony with a wave, not against it, and only if the wave is a significant one. His philosophy on accumulating stock is to buy on the down wave, ride through the small to medium rising waves until you see an especially strong breaking wave. Then sell.

Complete mastery of the Wyckoff method means working both sides of the waves — covering all shorts and going long at the bottom of a panic, depression or intermediate bear swing as well as selling out all long stocks and going short at the top of a boom or an intermediate bull movement.

In the Wyckoff method, determining these critical turning points is not so much using mathematics as it is gauging investor psychology. At the heart of Wyckoff's analysis is the knowledge that traders and investors are influenced by tips, news items, rumors, earnings analyses, financial reports, dividend rates and myriad other sources of information. It isn't important to Wyckoff which of these prompts a buy or sell order — all individual actions boil down to market behavior, as if the fluctuations were the result of one person's investment operation, a "composite" investor.

Wyckoff visualized this composite investor because he

FIGURE 1.3

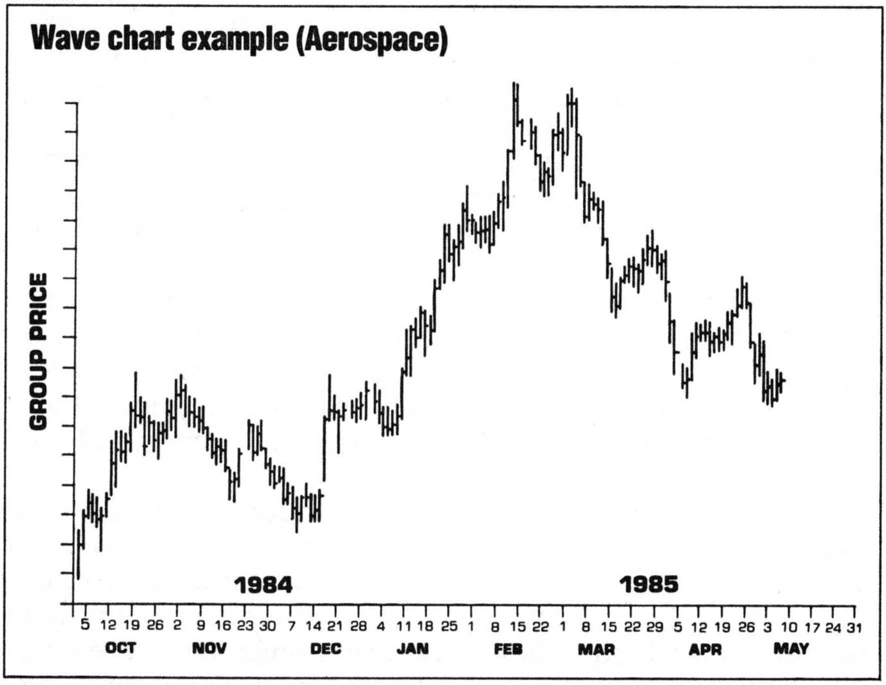

Select at least the top five stocks of an industry group and sum their prices to form a wave chart. This very selective chart often depicts the leaders in the stock market and thereby forewarns of changes in the composite averages.

knew there are "usually one or more large operators working in every stock. Sometimes there are many." In his day, wealthy individuals or well-informed insiders could fill the role. Today, insurance companies investing millions of premium dollars and institutional investors managing pension funds are "large operators" whose decisions affect the market simply by the magnitude of their investments.

Wyckoff studied his charts to uncover the motives of these large investors with enough capital to exert a force on the price of stocks and ultimately the entire market. He was not interested in their identity, only in their game plan. When large operators disclose their anticipation of price advances or declines with their purchases or sales, they signal possible future events in the market or in an individual stock.

Wyckoff's method is built on three basic types of charts — vertical line (bar), figure (point & figure), and one he developed, the wave chart. Vertical line charts (Figure 1.1) record an individual stock, group or composite average's high, low, and closing prices, and volume. From vertical line charts, investors following the Wyckoff method can determine the direction in which prices are moving, the most opportune time for buying, selling, or closing out, and at which prices to place their stop orders.

Figure (point & figure) charts (Figure 1.2) follow price changes only from one whole point to the next, focusing on price level while ignoring time. From these charts, the Wyckoff student forecasts the approximate number of points that a stock, a group of stocks or the composite averages should move.

Wyckoff's wave chart (Figure 1.3) records the aggregate price of at least five leading stocks much like stock index bar charts today. These choices are not permanent. The group is adjusted to include stocks that are continuously active in an industry and which indicate real leadership. The wave chart gives investors a means of detecting critical points in the market's travel from one wave to another, frequently warning of coming changes days before they are apparent in the composite averages.

At the very minimum, an investor experienced in the Wyckoff method can follow the stock market with a daily financial newspaper, a notebook and an hour a day in a quiet place. "The best results I ever had in judging the market and trading," writes Wyckoff, "were when I could devote only one hour a day to study the market, planning my campaigns, and giving instructions."

Obviously, investment capital isn't a prerequisite to studying the Wyckoff method. Practicing trades on paper is free, and Wyckoff is a staunch advocate of practice now or lose money in the long run. Even initiates who feel they have graduated from paper trading are advised by Wyckoff to begin their investing with small, equal lots of the three, five, 10, or 20 best stocks indicated by the charts.

Many times, as the years go by, we forget how or why we got to our current trading technique. Many times, too, an investor who wants to enter technical analysis is bewildered by the choices of methodology or unfamiliar with the principles guiding the schools of thought.

Wyckoff's method is valuable to either situation. In the next chapters, we will take you through it, step by step. We'll look in-depth at his charts, apply them to modern stock market activity, walk through each of his buying and selling tests and work on the finer points of market activity and actual transactions.

The aim of this book, as Wyckoff said, is to show you the "real" rules of the game.

2
Elements of Charting

The two most desirable things to know about the stock market are when the final top of a bull market, an intermediate swing or a minor move occurs and when the final bottom of a bear market, an intermediate swing or a minor move comes about.

Like everything else in stock market analysis, it's easier said than done. That's why the person who can accurately interpret charts to determine where the market lies at any given moment holds the key to successful trading and investing.

The forecasting value of charts is the focus they bring to supply and demand, trading volume and the urgency of trading—the forces that lift and depress prices. Charts tell an experienced reader whether the market, a group of stocks or any single stock is likely to advance, decline or stand still.

Richard Wyckoff believed that using charts mechanically, without judgment, is a practice headed for more failure than success. Drawing diagrams or imaginary geometrical patterns from charts or applying an arbitrary system of rules to their formations is anathema to the Wyckoff method. Instead, Wyckoff investors study charts to uncover the motives behind

FIGURE 2.1

This vertical chart records the monthly high, low, and close of the S&P 500 composite index. This chart provides a very long-term view of the direction of the stock market.

FIGURE 2.2

S&P 500 COMPOSITE SPOT INDEX, Weekly (1941-43 = 10)

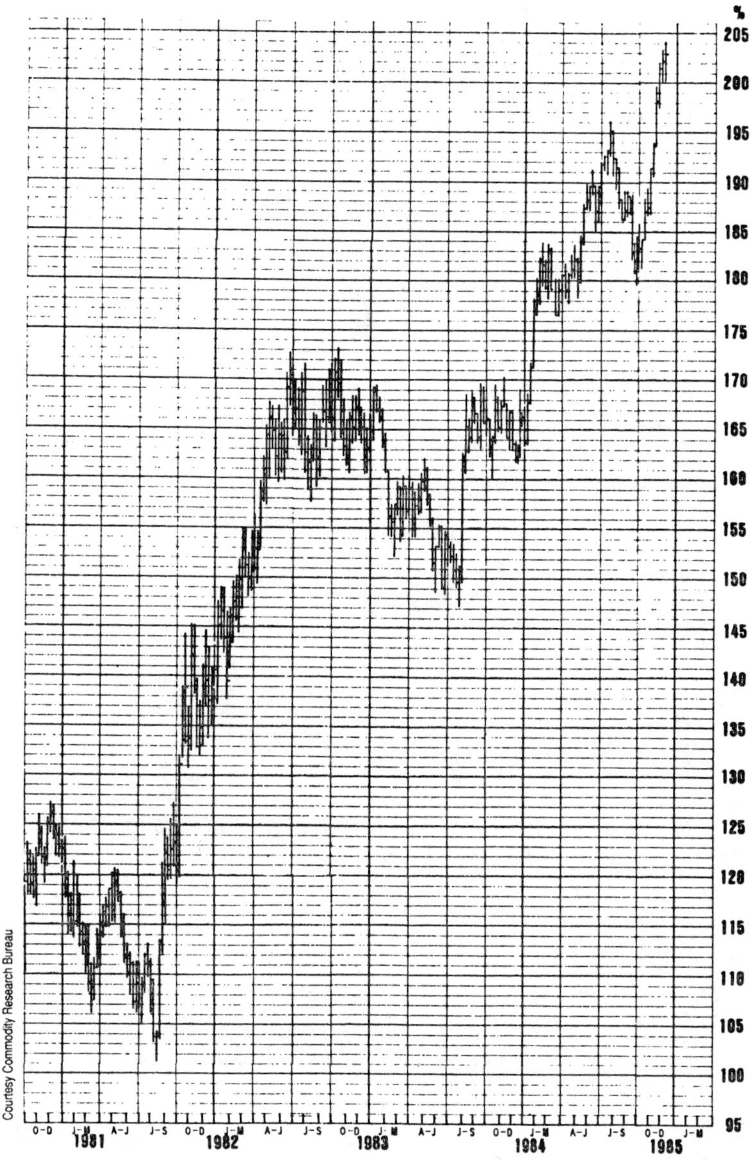

This vertical chart records the weekly high, low and close of the S&P 500 composite index. It is useful for highlighting the intermediate-term trends in the stock market.

FIGURE 2.3

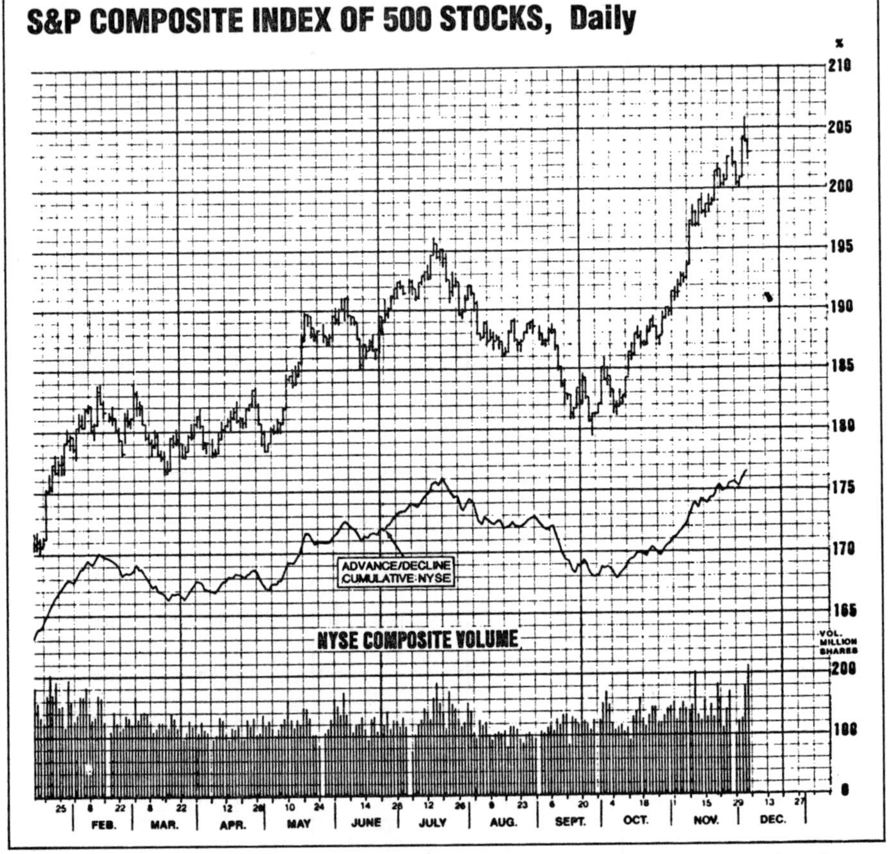

Courtesy Commodity Research Bureau

The daily vertical chart of the S&P 500 assists the trader in recognizing the short to intermediate price swings of the stock market.

market action to interpret the behavior of stocks.

The Wyckoff method relies on three basic types of charts: vertical line charts (bar charts), figure charts (points and figure charts), and wave charts, developed by Wyckoff in 1916 during his own career as a stock market analyst and trader. Each chart represents unique information that fits neatly with the others in a kind of symbiotic relationship.

Vertical charts (Figures 2.1-2.3) follow price and volume. They indicate the direction of price movement, whether it's a period to buy, sell or close out, and where to place stop orders.

Figure charts also follow price and volume, but in an abbreviated fashion. They indicate the best opportunities for profit by describing the distance an individual stock, a group of stocks or the market should move.

Wave charts (Figure 1.3) indicate the psychological moments to buy or sell. Wave charts look at the behavior of the market at critical points during minor, intermediate and major trends, and show their turning points.

An investor/trader could keep an overwhelming number of Wyckoff charts without a plan of action. But the method steps logically from charts of the entire market, to groups, and on to individual stocks. Investors/traders practiced in the Wyckoff method limit their chart work so the bulk of their time is devoted to studying and interpreting their records. At the same time, they still keep enough charts to give themselves selection and a broad perspective of the trends.

An introduction to the Wyckoff method starts with vertical and figure charts, which directly supplement each other. Vertical charts describe the direction in which a stock, a group or the market is headed, while figure charts indicate just how far they should go. Constructing these charts requires only graph paper and the stock report in the daily newspaper.

VERTICAL LINE CHARTS (BAR CHARTS)

Vertical charts record the daily high, low and closing prices plus the trading volumes of individual stocks, averages for groups of stocks or the market's leading composite averages, depending on their intended use.

A vertical chart for an individual stock, for instance, records each day's exact high, low and closing prices, including fractions, and joins them with a vertical line. Beneath the price lines, the day's trading volume sprouts from the bottom of the chart as another vertical line.

The price and volume lines show the day's tugging between bears and bulls, while the closing price indicates the result of the day's battle. When the closing prices are joined in a continuous line across the chart, they also indicate the net

FIGURE 2.4

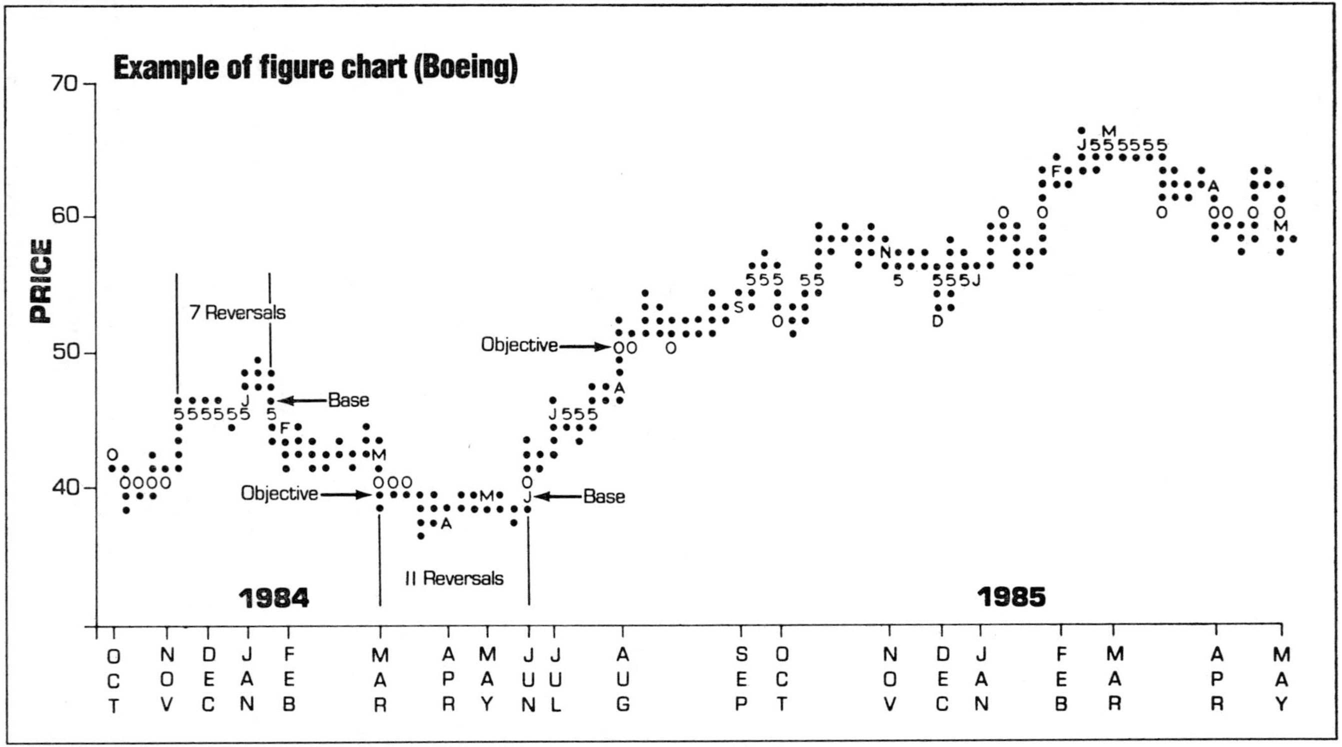

A figure chart records only the price movement of a stock that is greater than a minimum increment. In this one-point chart, the price movements of less than a full point are ignored. Price objectives are determined by counting the sideways movement in a base. The longer the sideways movement, the longer the subsequent trend. If the stock makes a total of 11 reversals within the base, then the price objective will be 11 points beyond the base.

progress of the market.

The price movement in a vertical chart indicates supply and demand, the points of resistance and support, and the trend, while changes in volume describe the intensity of the trading and the quality of the buying and selling. Together, price and volume signal the direction of coming moves—when a stock is on the springboard and ready to jump, when a move is culminating and whether this is the phase to buy or sell, go long or go short.

A daily vertical chart is sensitive to the most advantageous conditions for buying and selling and to turning points. When daily charts are condensed into weekly and monthly charts they visualize long-term trends and long-range moves to help the investor/trader judge the market's present position in relation to ultimate destination.

Vertical charts that record the market's leading composite averages are called trend charts. Two trends should be considered in trading: the immediate trend for active traders looking for profits in small swings, and the intermediate swings of five to 30 points that afford excellent opportunities for all trading and investing. These intermediate swings occur while the market is cycling from the upward trend of a bull market or the downward trend of a bear market and vice versa.

It's vital to know whether the intermediate swing is beginning, ending, partly over or in a period of transition, as well as whether the overall market is on an upswing or downswing. In an upward bull market, most of your trades should be on the long side and, in a declining bear market, orders should be on the short side. Going long in a bull market means that even if your stock declines, the market's upward trend will tend to return a profit if you have patience. If you go long in a bear market and miss the mark, your losses most likely will keep increasing.

A trend chart of the composite averages is the best way to determine what stage the market is in. It's a large-scale road map to judge the market's present position relative to its ultimate destination.

Of course, all stocks don't move up and down together.

They do tend to move downward more uniformly in declining markets. But when a declining market is ending, some stocks and some groups will stabilize and head upward before the rest, moving much faster and farther than the average.

Determining which groups of stocks show the most promise for profit entails group charts. Group charts are vertical charts that record the averages of at least five leading stocks in an industry or a market segment as you've defined it. Group charts point out the industries that promise to improve or deteriorate and cue you to search these groups for individual stocks.

A group chart is constructed by selecting the leading stocks in a group and calculating the averages of their highest, lowest and closing prices (i.e., add up all the highest prices and divide by the number of stocks to calculate the group's average closing price). Volumes are simply totaled, without dividing or averaging. These average prices and total volume are charted like any other vertical chart. Some group charts weight individual issues by the quantity of outstanding shares.

The goal is to compare your group charts with the market activity in your trend charts and find the groups that are strong when the market is weak or groups that are weak when the market is strong. The reason is simple: In a weak market, buyers obviously have reason to believe they can sell later at a higher price. On the other hand, a group that is exceptionally weak in a strong market indicates that somebody knows something to its disadvantage and is selling out. Whether the selling is out of urgency or profit-taking, the end result will be the same.

Figure charts (point & figure)

Figure charts record only the price movements from one whole number, or figure, to another. They don't recognize fractional price changes. Their value is in estimating the probable extent of supply and demand and the points of resistance and support.

Figure charts (Figure 2.4) are used in conjunction with vertical charts to more accurately map the future of a move. A vertical chart is like a compass pointing out the direction, while the figure chart shows how far it should go.

Figure charts contain only the amount of detail you want. One-point figure charts record every full price change — from 57 to 58 to 59. Three-point figure charts record only three-point changes — from 57 to 60 to 63. Five- and 10- point charts follow the same pattern.

The Wyckoff method requires experience with one- and three-point charts. The one-point chart indicates immediate or shorter-swing objectives, while the three-point chart is a guide to general trends and probable objectives of the large swings. Together, one- and three-point figure charts usually confirm each other, although if they differ markedly, the more conservative indication is chosen.

A one-point figure chart for a stock can be built from vertical charts or from the daily newspaper listings of opening, highest, lowest and closing prices.

Suppose your stock closed at 50 on Monday. On Tuesday it opened at 50 3/4, went as high as 51 7/8, as low as 45 3/ 4 and closed at 48 3/4.

Your one-point figure chart for the two days looks like this:

Tuesday's high—51	
Monday's close—50	
	49
	48 48—Tuesday's close
	47 47
	46—Tuesday's low

A three-point figure chart condenses the one-point chart by discarding all changes of less than three points. In our previous example, the only three-point move occurs between Tuesday's high and Tuesday's low. The three-point chart would look like:

One-point chart			Three-point chart
Tuesday's high—51			
Monday's open—50	50		50—Monday's open
	49		49
	48	48	48
	47	47	47
	46—Tuesday's low		46—Tuesday's low

The figure chart's general patterns detect accumulation or distribution, clearly mark lines of support and supply, and identify marking up and marking down periods.

However, the most valuable features of figure charts are their "horizontal formations" or sideways holding formations, which in many cases will approximate the number of points a single stock, a group of stocks or a market average should move. In addition, these horizontal formations, or "congestion areas," also help determine when a stock has met opposition and reached the end of its move.

So far, we've seen how vertical and figure charts show the direction and dimension of a move. In deciding when to act, a wave chart is the best guide.

WAVE CHARTS

A wave chart shows the psychological moment to buy or sell. It is the pulse of the market, a condensed picture of every vital development in every stock market session and an invaluable aid in determining the turning points of minor and intermediate swings — frequently days before the popular averages give an indication.

Wave charts are graphs of the aggregate price of the five leading stocks of an industry group over the past several months. This group of five is adjusted from time to time, so the wave chart shows the progress of stocks with continuous and real leadership. Every change in the aggregate price throughout the trading day is plotted, and a complete wave chart also shows volume and an index of activity, or intensity of trading.

We'll get into a complete discussion of wave charts a little later because mastery of them requires a thorough understanding of other concepts.

Chart building is, essentially, a clerical task, but one that can teach important lessons about market behavior. One trap to avoid is devoting more time to constructing charts than to interpreting them. It's a balance that comes with practice.

At the start, Wyckoff recommends maintaining trend charts of the market averages and group charts of the most important group averages. Then, when the group charts offer promising opportunities, refer to figure charts of individual stocks in that group to decide which are in the best position. When you've narrowed your selection to one or two of the best stocks in the group, it's a simple matter to make vertical charts of those stocks if you've kept a permanent file of the daily newspaper stock reports.

An additional tool for gauging where individual stocks are headed is the position sheet. A position sheet is a daily tally of your interpretation of each stock's figure and vertical charts. It summarizes whether you feel a stock is ready for a long or short upward or downward swing or whether there's no definite indication of a move either way. It is a cross-check on your chart interpretations and can eventually replace your group charts and help you judge the trend of the whole market.

Just keep in mind that when you're charting, you're dealing with waves. Every swing in the market, no matter how many points it is, consists of numerous buying and selling waves. The waves last just so long as they can attract a following and when that following is exhausted, the wave ends and a contrary wave sets in. It's much like the tide moving to a higher or lower level through a series of surges.

The small buy-sell waves during one day are part of larger waves that run several days and eventually turn into 3- to 5-point movements. These, in turn, become the 10- to 20-point waves that build into bear and bull markets.

By comparing the duration, the speed and the extent of these various waves, an investor/trader can judge the strength of the bears and the bulls as the market progresses and earn real profitability by working both the up and the down sides of the waves.

3
Market Trends in Composite Averages

Now that we've completed an overview of the history and philosophy behind the Wyckoff method and an outline of the procedures, let's start digging deeper into the actual techniques. Although we'll be concentrating on the stock market, these techniques are equally valid in the commodities, currencies, bond and precious metals markets.

Before you can master the Wyckoff method, however, you must remember that judgment is the most important technique. You must use your mind and your experience because there are no fixed and firm rules about market behavior — only general guidelines.

Keep two rules firmly in your mind, and you'll greatly increase your likelihood of success with the Wyckoff method. The first rule is this: Don't expect the market to behave exactly the same way twice. The market is an artist, not a computer. It has a repertoire of basic behavior patterns that it subtly modifies, combines and springs unexpectedly on its audience. A trading market is an entity with a mind of its own.

The second rule is this: Today's market behavior is significant only when it's compared to what the market did yesterday, last week, last month, even last year. There are no predetermined, never-fail levels where the market always changes. Everything the market does today must be compared to what it did before.

When we study the market, our ultimate quest is to determine when the current trend will change — either briefly or for the long term. Knowing a change is imminent tells us whether we should be trading on temporary declines and rallies or whether we should be investing for the long haul.

Every Wyckoff stock market analysis starts with a vertical line chart recording daily changes in a selected composite average. Almost any popular average printed each day in your local newspaper will work. I recommend using the Standard & Poor's Composite Index 500 Stocks in *The Wall Street Journal*. The vertical line chart of averages shows daily high and low prices connected by a vertical line and the closing price as a dash across the high-low line. Volume is another line sprouting from the bottom of the chart.

All these elements of price plus volume are necessary to gauge the market's behavior. One line doesn't tell the whole story. As David Weis, an expert in the Wyckoff method, says in his *Elliott Wave Commodity Letter*, "For me, studying a chart that does not include volume is like reading a road map without highway numbers." You need price and volume to determine if buyers' demand is more powerful than sellers' supply to know if the market can move upward and vice versa.

What can you learn from a composite average chart? You learn where the market is taking your groups of stocks and individual picks. You learn to recognize the first inklings of change and to look closely at your group and individual charts for complementary or conflicting signals.

No market moves smoothly upward or downward. Experienced operators are constantly testing the waters, and the market is a rolling sea of rallies, reactions, mark-ups, shakeouts, climaxes and turning points.

Let's look at the averages' fundamental behavior patterns

and how buyer-seller psychology brings them about. Then we'll see what they look like on an actual S&P 500 chart.

BEAR MARKET CORRECTION

We'll start with a market ready to end its decline. A declining market will always catch some investors/traders with high-priced stocks in their portfolios. Maybe they refused to sell because they thought the downturn would be short and temporary, or they bought during the decline in the hopes of a fast, profitable rally. Eventually, there comes a time when their hopes are dashed and they just want to unload their increasing losses.

This sets the stage for a selling climax, customarily followed by a technical rally (automatic rally or rebound) and secondary reaction (or test), and several opportunities to buy on the long side.

SELLING CLIMAX BOTTOMS

A selling climax is the finale to a panicky unloading of stocks, which are snapped up by more savvy operators. On a vertical line chart of a composite average, a selling climax is foretold by a sudden, abnormally large volume — sellers frantically unloading their losses. The price range usually drops and widens, the closing price hits nearer and nearer to the days showing a high volume and a closing price near the high (see Figure 3.1).

A technical rally follows, often caused by short covering. Volume dips and the price range jumps higher on the rally. To the uninitiated, the market seems to have instantly turned bullish. But in actuality, the ensuing secondary reaction will show where the market is really headed, because it will reveal what buyers were trying to accomplish during the selling climax.

If buyers during the climax did not intend to hold onto their purchases — perhaps they were large interests simply trying to shore up prices — then those stocks will be thrown back on the market at the first chance, normally the technical rally. If this new supply is too large for buyers to absorb, the market reacts with prices dropping lower than the extreme low re-

FIGURE 3.1

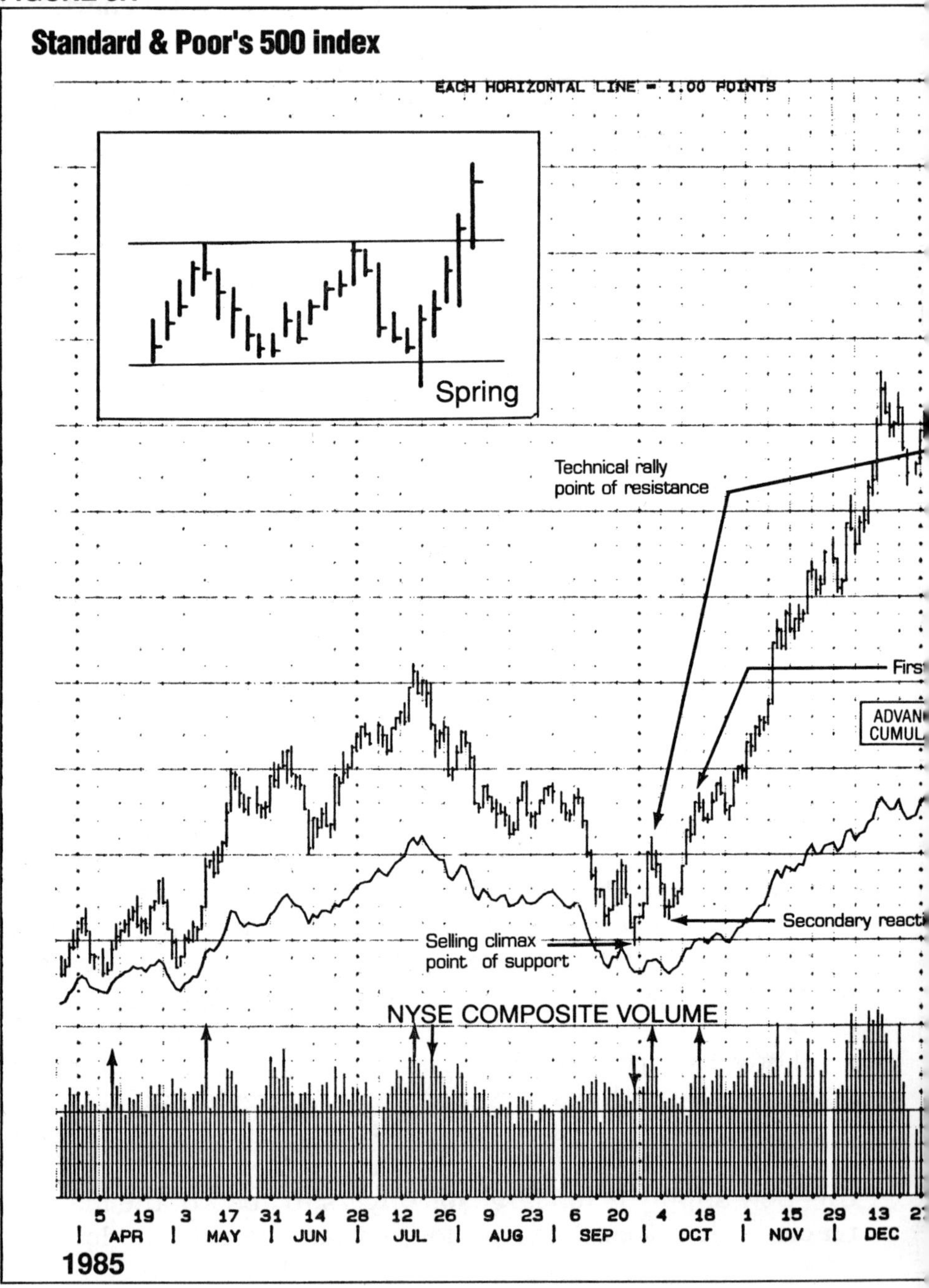

Chart courtesy Commodity Research Bureau

corded on the selling climax day, and a new decline is in the offing.

But if the market reacts to the rally with shrinking volume and the prices that hold at or above the selling climax's low, it's an indication that the selling spree has stabilized, buying power is again coming into the market and an upturn may be on the way.

This pattern of selling climax, technical rebound and secondary reaction occurs often in the large trend and in day-to-day movements. It can be a major event or minor glitch in the market's overall direction. But one selling climax invariably differs from the next. The heralding volume surge may last one day or several. It may hit on the day that prices reach their lowest point, or some days ahead of it. Again, the rules of judgment and comparison must be put into practice.

An experienced Wyckoff analyst who sees the selling climax's combination of excessive volume and extremely low price, followed by rallying prices and low volume, would look to the secondary reaction as the basis for the next forecast. If reaction prices held above the climax's low, it would indicate the decline had bottomed, and final confirmation of an important reversal would be prices rising above the technical rally's extreme high.

The rally's highest price is an important reference point, called a "point of resistance," because it is the most recent ceiling on price increases. Its counterpart is the "point of sup-

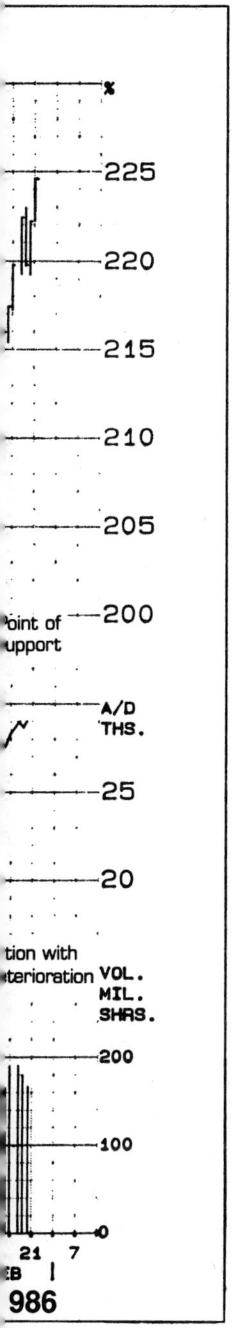

Figure 3.1
Typical bear market intermediate-trend cycle followed by a strong bull market intermediate-trend cycle. Each of these major phases (bull or bear) is separated by a short corrective phase.

port," the market's most recent, lowest price, the spot where prices stopped dropping lower. Breaching either the high, the point of resistance, or the low, the point of support — especially when volume is increasing — is a significant market achievement. Comparing current prices with these points is an important analytical tool, and placing stop orders near these points is a vital safety measure.

THE BULL MARKET

Three opportunities to buy long usually occur during the selling climax/technical rally/secondary reaction chain of events. The first is immediately after the climax, with a stop loss order placed two or three points under the purchase price and one to two points (about 3/4 to 1-1/2% of the price) under the low climax day. The second chance to buy long is after a secondary reaction, showing buyers are gaining the upper hand — characterized by retreating volume and prices hovering above the climax low. This type of reaction is said to broaden the "zone of support," and the average is on the "springboard," ready to advance. The third, but least favorable, chance to buy is if the average tops the technical rally's highest price, the point of resistance. Purchases are now on an upwave rather than a turning point and risk is materially increased. Stop loss sell orders must still be maintained below both the recent selling climax point of support and secondary reaction low point. These low points may be tested several times before a bull market begins. The longer this period of testing, sideways or dullness persists, the more likely the resulting price move will be significant.

A market just starting an upward climb is ripe for a buying climax and a corrective downswing. Clues that a buying climax and downswing are surfacing: daily highs that barely move higher, indicating buyers are reluctant to follow prices up; closing prices that barely fluctuate from one day to the next; and volume that tapers off, indicating lessening demand. Like a selling climax, a buying climax is characterized by a sudden increase in volume. When the high-volume day sets a new high yet closes near the low, a correction is in the offing.

When the price range begins to drop, analysts watch for signs that the market will be able to pull out of the corrective decline. Diminishing volume on declining prices is a bullish sign that sellers are not pressuring the market. When a session during the correction closes near its high, it's both a sign the correction is nearly over and a new buying opportunity. True bullish behavior resumes when the price ranges and closing prices move higher and are accompanied by gradually increasing volume.

As the rising closing prices climb nearer and nearer the last point of resistance, the market's natural reaction is to hesitate. The average fluctuates within a narrow range because it is absorbing the offerings of over-anxious buyers who got hooked near the last high point and are eager to get out even.

This absorption or accumulation process can be distinguished from its opposite, the distribution process, by several factors: When prices hit the low end of the narrow trading range, volume remains low; the low end of the trading range is less than halfway to the market's last point of support; and as the lows again start to move upward, volume consistently increases — typical behavior at the end of an accumulation period prior to a mark-up.

During a mark-up phase, the average quickly gains a large number of points and volume likewise rockets. After this steep rise, the average may hesitate in a narrow range. Again, watch the lows — the supporting zone — of this hesitation, and volume's reaction for a clue to coming events. If volume promptly decreases when the low dips, it says the market isn't ready to turn downward, and another advance is coming.

A lasting advance will send prices higher with proportional volume increases. If price makes smaller advances on increasing volume, then the market is warning of a distribution period. The advance has lured the public into buying, and large operators can profitably unload, or distribute, their holdings. The climactic signal for the distribution period is, again, a sharp volume increase and price upthrust that warns that stops should be moved closer to recent lows in preparation for a reaction.

BULL MARKET CORRECTION

The reaction — a drop in trading range and closing price while volume stays high — indicates that the large operators are still unloading and their supply is overcoming demand. If the market had advanced significantly before distribution set in, the reaction may be severe and even constitute a turning point. Comparing the behavior of this volume with that of previous reactions puts the magnitude of supply into perspective. Whether or not an impending, significant reaction looks like a turning point, it is time to close out all long trading positions and go short to profit from the downturn.

Wyckoff also advocates liquidating investments and standing aside while the market works out such a serious downswing. Even though the reaction may be temporary, he argues, its severity could significantly depreciate investment and some of the investments might not recover in an ensuing advance. With buying power intact, investment positions can be re-established when the market gives warning that it is bullish again.

Like an advancing market that tests previous highs, a declining market generally will test previous lows, and a sharp decline toward the support level almost assures an attempt at a rally; some buyers will feel that stocks are cheap again and bearish traders will buy out their short positions.

The question in a case like this is, How high can the rally go? Is it lasting or temporary? Large operators aren't likely to let the average immediately go back to the former highs where they unloaded large volumes. They'd just as soon let buyers at the former highs get tired of holding on to losses and then let prices run — if they felt prices could go substantially above the former level. They would need a substantial run-up to ensure themselves a profit on the stocks they would have to buy back from those who bought at the former highs.

More likely, the large operators would attempt just enough of a rally to keep the buyers of their original large-volume sales locked in and to discourage amateur shorts from selling, while they unload even more stock on the new, lower rally. This kind of move is apparent if the average rises halfway to its previous high but volume isn't increasing the way it did during the previous high advance. This says that buyers are filled up and the large operators are attempting to bid up prices; the rally is purely technical, supply is outdistancing demand and it is time to take short positions.

Attempts at rallying may persist, but after more than one period of distribution, the average is most likely in a critical position. Unless unseen buyer demand is waiting in the wings, a decline proportional to the distribution period is the offing.

Bear market

A test of buying power comes as the average heads downward toward a supporting point. On steadily expanding volume, it's very unlikely the supporting point will hold. Too much is being offered to buyers who have bought all they can afford.

Although declining prices accompanied by a persistent increase in volume is characteristic of a liquidating market, it may be pockmarked by occasional, sharp rallies on markedly decreased volume. These rallies are quickly lost because their driving power is short-covering, not solid demand. Rather than pointing to possible upturns, these brief rallies with their immediate drop in volume simply affirm the weak buying power.

When looking only at an average, its rate of decline is a key to its fortune. A slowing of the decline may be the average's only warning of a turning point. A slowing of the decline accompanied by comparatively heavy volume warns that a minor turning point could be ahead and could be the precursor of an important change. If the rally is quick and violent, however, experience says it is not the stuff of lasting trend reversals but may set a new supporting point and open a chance for trading long with very close stops. The question is whether large operators will dump a new supply on the rally's buying power and drown it.

After prices have begun to rally, a buying climax or shortened upthrusts on declining demand are bearish signs. Yet prices may still bid up to a new high to catch shorts and make room for large and experienced operators to sell on the impending decline. At this point, sideways movement of the average on declining volume would show lessening demand at the top of the rise, and further sideways motion would definitely break the rally's stride. Narrowing price ranges, lower closings and less volume indicate the market is saturated with offerings and buying power has lessened. This is known as the last point of supply from which the market begins its markdown. At this point, distribution is complete, and going short would carry the least risk.

When a market is heading for a serious decline, the public can be lulled into indifference and misinterpretation by volumes that are relatively smaller than volumes in advancing markets. The reason is psychological. Most buyers are attuned to advancing markets and understand how profits can be taken when prices are increasing. Because they fear to sell short, they don't participate in the declining markets. This makes volume relatively lighter and trading a professional affair.

A market, however, will seldom run continuously in one direction without some sort of reversal. Each time the average nears former supporting points, it signals where it is headed. Either it rebounds and establishes a new support point or breaks through to new or earlier support levels. A long decline without serious interruption puts the market in an oversold condition and a sharp rebound would be expected. But again, a rally that is too effervescent is not likely to last — it is merely short-covering at once, and liquidation is likely to resume.

A long decline in the average may give only subtle signals of impending change. An accelerated decline after a significant drop in the average is a warning to be wary. If followed by what looks to be a selling climax — a sharp increase in volume and higher closing — it may prove to be a shake-out. A trader should not jump to the conclusion that a violent recovery is on the way, but it would be time to cover shorts and closely monitor the average for rally and reaction — especially the ability to hold at former support points or steady at a new price range.

A trader will look for opportunities to go long at the end of the reaction. This end is signaled by a higher low, higher closing and decreased volume. An upward climb will test previous resistance points and the reaction will give more important insight into the possibility of a new support level or a resumption of the bear market.

The average's ability to bounce off former support points will indicate buying power is coming back into the market. But it still would be logical to hold off on investments until a period of shortened price ranges, a so-called period of "dullness," indicates that a real bull market is being prepared.

4
Understanding Group Stock Behavior

The Wyckoff method of trading brings to the technical analyst a clean, logical way to understand stock market behavior and to anticipate the most opportune trading investment moments. The Wyckoff analyst begins with charts of a broad composite market average, overlays charts of industry group averages and then, when that information is weighed, compares the trends and critical turning points to the charts of individual stocks within the industry group.

Analyzing group averages is a vital step, because to go after individual stocks willy-nilly, without a plan of action, is to invite disaster or, at the very least, less than peak use of investment capital. Group behavior guides a trader to the appropriate section of the market where individual stocks should be selected.

Group averages compared with broad market trends will show you where large-scale traders see something promising and are trading accordingly. By using these signals to make well-timed long or short trades in conjunction with the safety

FIGURE 4.1

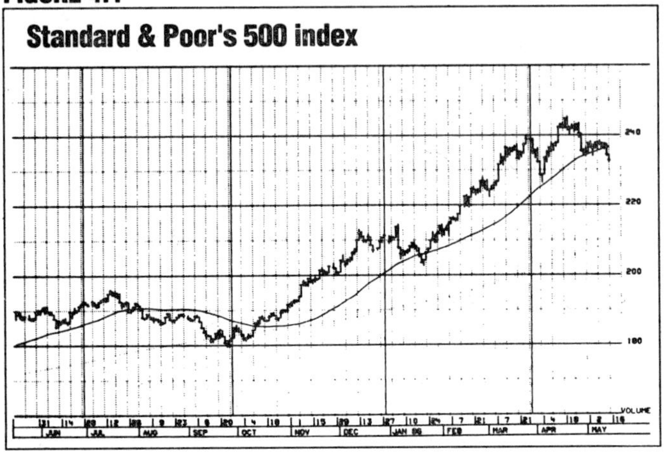

The S&P 500 composite index is making higher highs and higher lows, indicating a bull market from October to April. During January the trend became questionable when the market moved temporarily below the December lows.

FIGURE 4.2

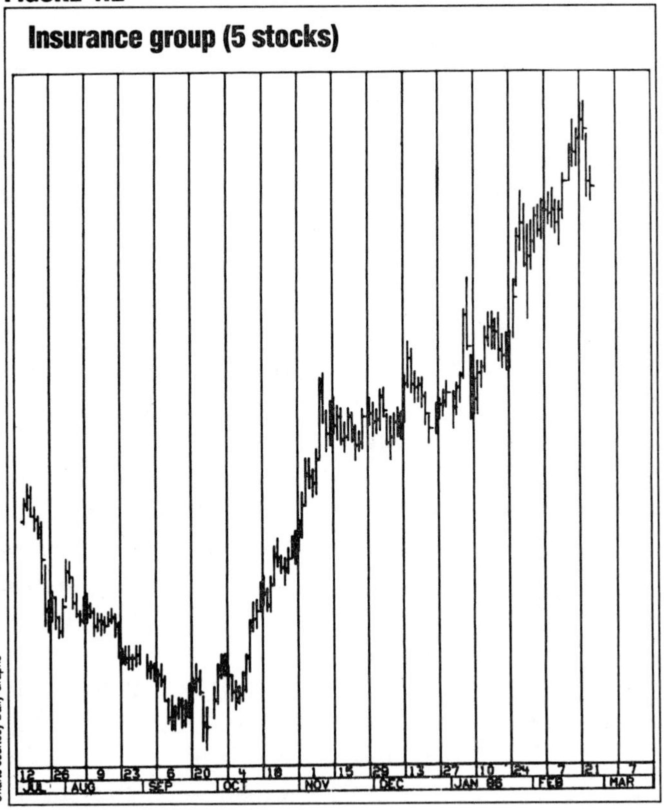

During January, the insurance group holds above its December lows while the S&P 500 did not. This was a positive sign regarding the technical strength of the insurance group.

Charts courtesy Daily Graphs

of stop orders, you can make both the up and down sides of the stock market profitable.

In a bull market, the Wyckoff analyst looks for group averages that are "strong" when the composite average hits "weak" spots. A strong group average hits a downwave. This resistance signifies that the group should be the fastest and highest rebounder when the market comes out of its slump. Looking behind the scenes, the resistance says the professional, large-scale operators are buying shares in this group while the market is relatively low because they anticipate significant gains in the future.

In a bear market, the best choice for selling short becomes a group that is "weak" when the market makes a rebound. The weak group is characterized by its feeble response to the composite average's rallies. The weakness indicates that the professionals know something that is to the group's disadvantage and are forcing shares on the market or testing the market to see if it can absorb a large volume of shares. In either case, the group's inability to rally along with the market targets it as a candidate for further declines and a place where short orders seem logical.

The testing in which large operators engage allows them to find out directly whether buying or selling is easiest in the current market. Since few individuals have the resources to run this sort of test, the best option is to look for signs of the operators' presence in the composite and group averages, decide whether they anticipate buying or selling, and follow in their footsteps.

In your composite and group comparisons you want to find the leading groups that will move first, fastest, and farthest. You aim to buy long in groups that resist the pull of bull market downwaves because this is where professionals are buying in anticipation of future upturns. You want to place short orders in groups that resist advancing when a bear market turns upward because the pros either see trouble on the horizon or the chance to buy in later at lower prices.

PROCESS OF ROTATION

This is not to say that just any stock in a favored group will yield the results you want. Just as groups of stocks do not rise and fall in harmony, neither do individual stocks. One group or stock may be leading the way up or down while another is still preparing to move. When the leading group or stock meets resistance that stymies its progress, the demand for buying or supply for selling will shift to another group or stock. This is the process of rotation that large-scale operators use to their advantage and also explains why dealing in the leaders will still leave time to catch the not-so-aggressive issues.

Wyckoff's process of rotation is based on the fact that all stocks do not move together at all times or in agreement with the prevailing trend. He observed that bull markets normally advance with high-priced, blue chip stocks as their leaders. These represent the more stable, financially solvent, and widely held stocks. Large operators include well-heeled individuals, insurance companies, corporations, and well-funded managers. These big interests can well afford the effort to examine a great deal of fundamental news information as well as the technical analysis tools and the money to price test the market. As the larger interest operators coax the price of the blue chip market leaders upward, the smaller, independent operators start to influence other issues that are more in line with their smaller financial ability to underwrite. Eventually, the general public will be attracted by this seemingly across-the-board bullish activity and be interested in lower-priced and more speculative issues. This is an example of the process of rotation and an explanation of why the blue chip stocks tend to such issues as over-the-counter stocks.

The process of rotation operates much the same way in bull and bear markets. In a bull market, a group may advance more rapidly than the market, then rest and go through a technical reaction. Demand then shifts to other groups making their advances. This explains why a group that has gone through a prolonged rise will begin a mixed price movement. Large-scale professionals are winding up their campaigns because they feel professionals are winding up their campaigns because

FIGURE 4.3

AETNA Life & Casualty

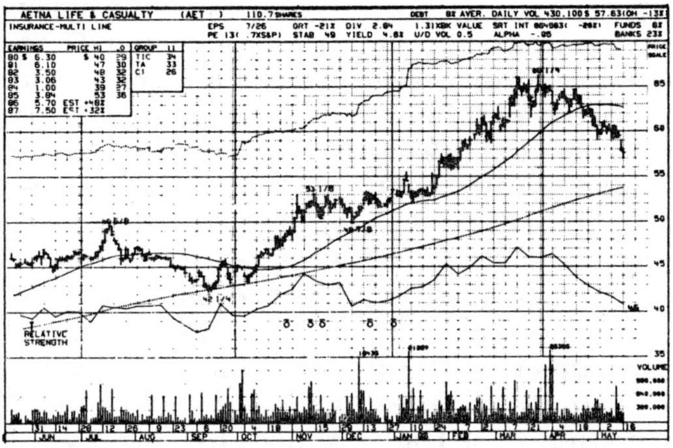

Chart courtesy Daily Graphs

Aetna stock was a leader during the bull phase, as indicated by its ability to stay well above the December lows in January. However, during April, Aetna lost its leadership role as it began to underperform the S&P 500, indicated by the lagging relative strength line.

they feel the group has reached its maximum profitability and are turning their attention to the laggards that still have room for advancement.

Supply moves similarly through groups in a bear market—only faster. This is because profit-taking retards upward movement in a bull market, but in a falling market the many untrained investors that make up the public hang onto their stocks until their last shred of hope is gone and then they rush in to sell their stocks without regard to value.

Let's take a look at how large-scale traders capable of influencing the market can use the process of rotation to their advantage. One way rotation aids large operators is by camouflaging their campaigns. When a stock leading the way in a falling market hits a turning point, the process of rotation states that selling will move to other groups and issues. Traders may then buy back previously sold-out leading stocks under the guise of rotational weakness without bidding up prices. This professional buyback occurs as the public gets out in panic or stays out of the market altogether.

Conversely, when a stock leading the way in a rising market comes to a turning point, the rotation of demand enables large traders to unload their other stocks under the cover of this rotational activity without forcing sales on the market and letting the air out of prices.

Professionals with the clout of large volumes also may keep their campaigns alive by invoking the process of rotation. They rapidly bid up prices of easily influenced stocks to keep the public in a buoyant, buying mood. You'll know when they've exhausted market demand because stocks respond sluggishly or fall back quickly after a leader has been "whooped up." Similarly, you can recognize when supply in a falling market is losing ground if the leader refuses to move lower as selling rotates to other stocks.

The process of rotation also helps explain why certain groups will be more bullish or bearish than their counterparts. But actually measuring the bullish strength or bearish weakness in a group requires attention to points of resistance and support.

To illustrate, a typical group in an advancing market may rise faster or higher than the composite average, then hit a normal period of leveling off (a "period of consolidation" or "hesitation"), followed by a reaction that drops the group average toward its previous low point. If the composite also is dropping and the group holds itself above or around the previous low, then the group is signaling strength and should be a leader when the composite resumes its upwave.

On the composite average's upwave, the group may reach new highs, but even more informative is the way the group handles itself during successive downwaves. An ascending line of low points is particularly noteworthy of strength. A tendency to react less than the market on a downwave also distinguishes technical corrections from the beginning of a bear trend and could be marking a turning point that other groups will join as the process of rotation works through them.

Sooner or later, however, the process of rotation catches up with the group and it loses its bullish strength. A frequent signal that a group is switching from strength to weakness is a more extensive drop during a technical reaction than the group has experienced before. When that drop is followed by a sluggish rally and a lower top in the face of a rising composite average, it pretty well confirms the switch.

Although demand in this one group has been played out, other groups can still be advancing or holding steady to offer more investment and trading opportunities. Of course, if the bull market continues long enough, the original, leading group can even rotate back into favor.

How long the rotational process continues depends on how long the market can sustain its trend — and groups will give early warning signals about that, too. If one group's deep reaction and sluggish rally signals that it is losing strength, then the sluggish response of most or all groups to the composite average's upwaves is a sign that the entire market is turning bearish.

Even facing a bear market, a trader/investor knows that the process of rotation will continue to operate, although at a faster pace. By simply reversing the technical considerations learned in a bull market, the trader has ample tools to make the best of the short side.

Always keep the process of rotation in mind while using the comparative power of group and composite charts. Make it a point never to get so caught up in comparing group leaders to the market that you ignore what the lagging groups are trying to tell you. Ignoring how the laggards are meeting their points of support and resistance can mean not only missed trading opportunities, but also missed warning signals about the market trend and the validity of your overall strategy.

5
Prelude to Individual Chart Reading

Averages — both market and group averages — are essential to stock market analysis and your investment or trading strategy using the Wyckoff method. But the true test of analysis begins when we move from market and group averages into the third stage of chart interpretation — the charts of individual stocks.

This is where a trader/investor absolutely must learn the fine points of market operation and technical indicators. There's no more "averaging" here, no margin for sloppy interpretation. Your money and, yes, your reputation are now on the line.

Unlike averages, stocks have personalities that can be unique. One stock may be a large investor's personal favorite, another may be the object of competition, and then there's always the forgotten waif waiting for the chance to show its stuff. But the beauty of the Wyckoff method is that it discerns these personalities and shows a trader/investor how to anticipate individual moods and reactions.

It does this because the charts of individual stocks are like the graphic waves on an oscilloscope screen. Both are windows into events we can't actually see as they're taking place. An oscilloscope doesn't show us individual electrons bouncing through a circuit, and a vertical chart doesn't peer into the offices of influential traders and investors. But if we know how to read them, both will show us where and how the influence — either electrical or monetary — is headed.

It's critical, therefore, that you completely understand how operators with large amounts of capital work the market. They have the time to investigate individual stocks and the capital to make things happen. What you're aiming to do is ride piggyback on their moves and share in the profits they intend to make for themselves.

When a large operator decides there's worthwhile profitability in a stock, you can pretty well divide the campaign into four phases that take place through both advancing and declining markets.

First there's "accumulation," the period of manipulation where an operator will bid low, gradually buy and sell, and buy again to acquire a line of stock at the lowest possible prices. The "marking up" phase follows when the operator ceases manipulations that kept prices low and allows the price to rise or gives it a push with well-placed bids. The operator acts as the issue's buying underwriter.

Once the public is aware of the "hot" rising stock, it's time for "distribution," or selling the line of stock. As prices peak, the operator may start "marking down" in preparation for a decline in the stock's price and the chance to make profits using short sales.

You can look at this manipulative process as a kind of investment "physics." The investment forces are supply and demand, and they can be pent up and released just like physical forces.

During the accumulation phase, a stock stores up the force of demand — supply grows scarce and demand builds, thus giving price the power to rise during the marking-up period and the momentum to keep rising before distribution sets in.

Distribution reverses the forces of supply and demand. As the operator puts the line of accumulated stock on the market, demand is assuaged and the power balance shifts in favor of marking down. In marking down, price falls until the selling out momentum is exhausted or a fresh force of demand overcomes it.

Interpreting and understanding these phases as they unfold on a chart can be accomplished only when price and volume are considered together.

PRICE VS. VOLUME STUDIES

Price alone tells the analyst what the stock's present technical position is and where the trend is probably headed. Volume determines the trend with more accuracy and detects turning points when to open or close trades, and when to change stop orders. Together, they form a complete picture.

Price and volume are linked much like a car and gasoline. Volume is to price what gasoline is to a car. The more gas you feed a car, the greater its momentum. Push in the clutch and the car coasts on its accumulated power. Give the accelerator just a tap, and the car doesn't roll as far.

Likewise, volume that expands consistently, growing larger and larger with public participation, gives price a momentum that's not readily reversed. Even when large operators stop their manipulations, the momentum of public participation carries on the price trend. But a temporary volume increase, like a tap on an accelerator, gives price a little boost that dies out quickly.

Price-volume relationships are not fixed; there are too many exceptions in the stock market. A Wyckoff analyst knows there are no unshakeable rules, no absolutely reproducible results. The Wyckoff analyst develops a "feel" for price-volume relationships the same way you develop a "feel" for your car's handling, and learns how to interpret current signals from the behaviors of the past.

When a Wyckoff analyst looks at the current price of a stock, he or she immediately compares it to previous prices where buyers supported a declining price or resisted paying more for an advancing stock. Whether a stock price can breach these support or resistance points is an essential clue to its future performance, and the support or resistance prices themselves are "danger points" that dictate where the stop orders should be placed.

Another essential test is how far a price drops during a reaction (the temporary decline after a bull market advance) or how far a price rises during a rally (the temporary advance after a bear market decline). This movement determines a stock's technical strength or weakness and, thus, its ability to continue its trend.

A "normal" reaction is half the distance of an advance. For example, after a 10-point advance, a normal reaction would be five points. Less than five points says the stock is in strong hands and likely to continue its climb. More than five points says the stock is in weak hands and the trend may be fading.

Conversely, after a 10-point decline, a less-than-5-point rally indicates technical weakness and a greater-than-5-point rally shows technical strength.

The analyst reading the vertical chart also is gauging the rate of price acceleration or deceleration and is looking for sudden, sharp up or down movements (called thrusts and shakeouts) or a price that stops oscillating and comes to "dead center."

This dead center or "hinge" price tells the analyst the stock may very well be "on the springboard," which is the best time of all to buy into a stock. When a stock is on the springboard, it's ready for sharp and immediate action. Entry into the market here makes most efficient use of your capital. The stock is no longer dilly-dallying around. It's ready to take off.

Springboards occur at the bottom of a range of accumulation or in the upper levels of a range of distribution.

On the bull side, a springboard will show up after the price has stayed in a trading range — either because a previous advance is being "consolidated" or "digested" or a new markup is under way. Usually, a springboard occurs at the bottom of a decline during the consolidation period because this is where operators are more likely to want to accumulate the stock for a bull campaign.

On the bear side, a stock is said to be on the springboard after preparations for distribution. A springboard will become evident after the price has declined and then stayed in a range. The springboard comes at the top of an advance during this preparation, a precursor of further distribution and plunging prices.

When a rising price tends to flatten out or "arch over," demand is dying or encountering a greater force of supply. When a declining price levels off or "rounds upward," it's telling the analyst that supply is petering out.

Of course, volume studies will confirm or deny these price clues and volume also is judged against its past behavior. The sheer magnitude of a stock on the market is not what draws an analyst's attention, but rather if the current volume magnitude is significantly different from preceding volumes.

A gradual volume buildup says the public is coming into an advancing market or leaving a declining one. Gradual volume growth is like a steadily pressed accelerator and gives price its momentum to continue advancing or declining.

An abnormally large or swift volume expansion during an advance or decline marks a turning point that's either temporary or lasting, depending on the stock's technical position.

A small volume, on the other hand, is like the end of a chapter in a book: a new chapter will begin sooner or later. Where the small volume occurs is the clue to the next phase.

A small volume at the bottom of a decline of any size indicates that selling is drying up and taking pressure off the decline. For example, when volume narrows and continues to fade away during a reaction, it says not much of the stock is for sale, even at lower prices, and the price should resume its advance.

Light volume at the top of a rally or a rise in price is often bearish because it says demand has been filled and without active demand, price goes lower.

But again, these are generalities. A stock's behavior has to be judged against its history and its unique personality. Isolating incidents on a chart and applying "rules" to them

FIGURE 5.1

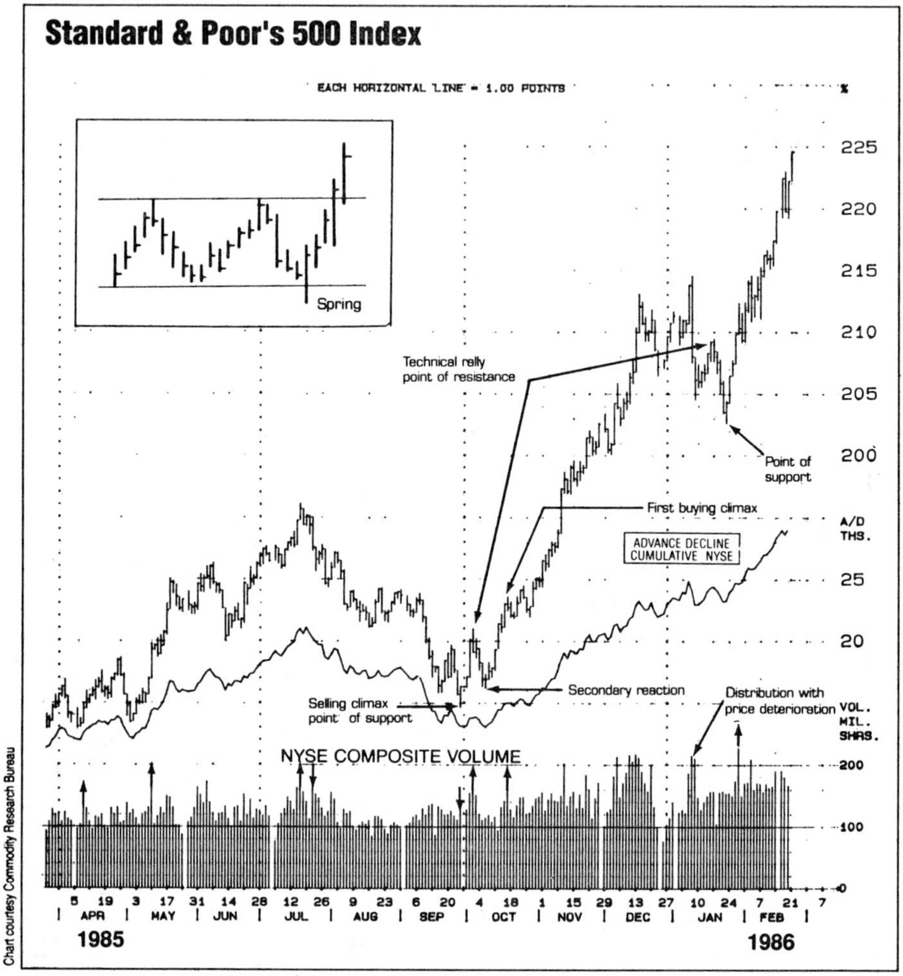

A spring occurs after a market has moved below a previous support point and fails to continue lower. This inability to move lower is created by a transfer of ownership from weak sellers to strong buyers. Typically, the price move after a spring is very swift.

invariably leads to disappointing results. The best teacher is charting the market, its groups and individual stocks without actually investing (paper trading). The nuances of price-volume relationships will unfold as your charts take shape and the experience will clearly register the concepts in your mind.

You shouldn't feel as though you must instantly recognize a campaign. Accumulation doesn't occur overnight. It takes considerable preparation to buy thousands or hundreds of thousands of shares without alerting every trader on the floor to what's going on and sending prices sky high.

THE CAMPAIGN

Usually, a large operator who finds reason to accumulate a stock tries to make that issue look unattractive by bidding low, buying a portion, offering part of that for sale, and finally buying more shares back. Accumulation comes across on vertical charts as a "congestion area" where prices stay in a certain range, moving "sideways" across the chart and showing no tendency to take off in either direction, accompanied by consistently low volume.

The prolonged process may even include some drastic downturns to shake stock out of tight-fisted owners' hands and into the operators' portfolio. The intentionally cloudy signals may not come into sharp focus until weeks or months have passed.

When the operator has all of the targeted stock in hand, the stage is set to "mark up" the price. This may be done gradually or swiftly, timed to coincide with favorable news from the corporation issuing the stock or let loose as the market takes off. Essentially, in marking up, the operator ceases the buying and selling gambit that kept prices depressed and lets outside demand begin to take over. On a vertical chart, marking up is a series of fast price upthrusts alternating with monetary plateaus or "resting spells," accompanied by rising volume.

The initial demand almost always comes from professional traders and investors because they are closest to the market. But to really reach a profit objective, an operator has to attract public attention and public buying . So distribution, or selling the accumulated line of stock, calls for manipulation, too.

Here, the operator uses the same kind of tactics — buying and selling from the accumulated line to give the stock an appearance of strength that induces public buyers into the market. The price can be barked up more than once, and a return of the characteristic congestion area on the vertical chart is evidence of important distributive selling. At the climax of distribution, a congestion area can signal that the move is ending and the operator is going short.

When an operator has unloaded the accumulated line, the stock is said to be "technically weak" or "overbought." Saying it's in "weak" hands means it's held mainly by public buyers who got in during or at the top of rising prices and can't or won't hang onto the stock when the price doesn't surge again. An overbought condition is especially prevalent when the price rises too rapidly and without corrective reactions or resting spells. In this condition, the price becomes sensitive to sales and the withdrawal of experienced buyers.

As we said before, when distribution is over, the operator again makes the price swing back and forth in a certain range, or congestion area, to fool the public into thinking the stock is waiting to take off again, while the operator takes a short position. Seeing that it's advantageous to "mark down" the price, the operator ceases the supporting manipulation, the professionals raid the stock, and the operator covers the short sales.

Once accomplished, the stock is said to be "technically strong" or "oversold." All those who could be induced to sell have done so, and the stock is in the hands of experienced operators.

6
Figure Charts

The price-volume information supplied by vertical charts are the mainstay of Wyckoff's . But as an adjunct to vertical charts, most Wyckoff analysts also employ figure charts, which record only price movement.

Figure charting allows the analyst to quickly see where and how strongly supply or support is building and to calculate the actual distance a priceshould rise or fall. Therefore, with a vertical chart pointing out direction, the figure chart shows just how far that direction should travel.

Figure charts are useful for market averages, group averages, and individual stocks. One-point figure charts ignore fractional price changes and record only full-figure price changes during a day's trading — for example, from 57 to 58 to 59. Three-point figure charts record only changes of three points or more — from 57 to 60 to 63. Five-point and 10-point charts follow the same pattern.

A one-point figure chart for a stock can be built from its vertical chart or from the daily newspaper listings of opening, highest, lowest, and closing prices. Figure charts are usually constructed as each vertical chart is constructed, although veteran Wyckoff analysts will watch for interesting developments in their figure charts before constructing the more detailed vertical chart.

Taking a quick look at how a figure chart is developed, suppose your stock closed at 50 on Monday. On Tuesday, it opened at 50 3/4, went as high as 51 7/8, as low as 45 3/4, and closed at 48 1/4.

Your one-point figure chart for the two days looks like this:

Tuesday's high—51		
Monday's high—50		
	50	
	49	
	48	48—Tuesday's close
	47	47
	46—Tuesday's low	

A three-point figure chart would condense the one-point chart by discarding all changes of less than three points. In our example, the only three-point move occurs between Tuesday's high and Tuesday's low. The three-point chart would look like this:

One-point chart			Three-point chart
Tuesday's high—	51		
Monday's close—	50	50	50—Monday's open
		49	49
	48	48	48
	47	47	47
Tuesday's low—	46		46

A figure chart's valuable feature is its horizontal formations —horizontal price lines that show where and how strongly the forces of demand and supply are gathering. Horizontal formations are easiest to discern when you step back, take in the entire figure chart, and notice where rallies and reactions begin growing.

In this hypothetical one-point figure chart, horizontal

formations clearly unfold at the 60 and 61 levels:

64										
63							63		63	
62	62						62	62	62	
61	61	61		61		61	61	61	61	—horizontal formation
	60	60	60	60	60	60	60	60	60	—horizontal formation
		59	59		59					

You can think of a horizontal formation as a kind of foundation or baseline on which significant activity builds. Without this horizontal baseline, there isn't much chance of prolonged price increase or decrease because either demand or supply is missing.

Experience says that the number of times a figure is repeated in a horizontal formation is the number of points a stock, group, or the market average will advance from its deepest low or decline from its peak high. Counting the width of a horizontal formation includes both numbers and blank spaces between numbers. In the example above, the horizontal formation at 61 is 10 figures wide — eight numbers and two spaces.

A horizontal formation after a decline indicates that operators are willing to support the stock and stem the decline. After a rally, a horizontal formation uncovers the supply that's being offered and signals a downturn in prices as soon as the supply satiates demand.

If the stock in our previous example had already been through a markdown, we'd assume the horizontal formations at 60 and 61 were demand lines and heralded a rise. To calculate how far the price could rise, we would add the horizontal formation's width of 10 to the bottom price or 59 and expect the price ultimately to hit 69. Of course, we would continue to test the accuracy of this calculation as further activity was recorded on the figure chart — particularly if other, wider horizontal formations became

Figure 6.1 *(see next page) A figure chart pattern is often based on a consolidation pattern that has a specific trading rule for a buy or sell signal.*

FIGURE 6.1
Figure chart formations

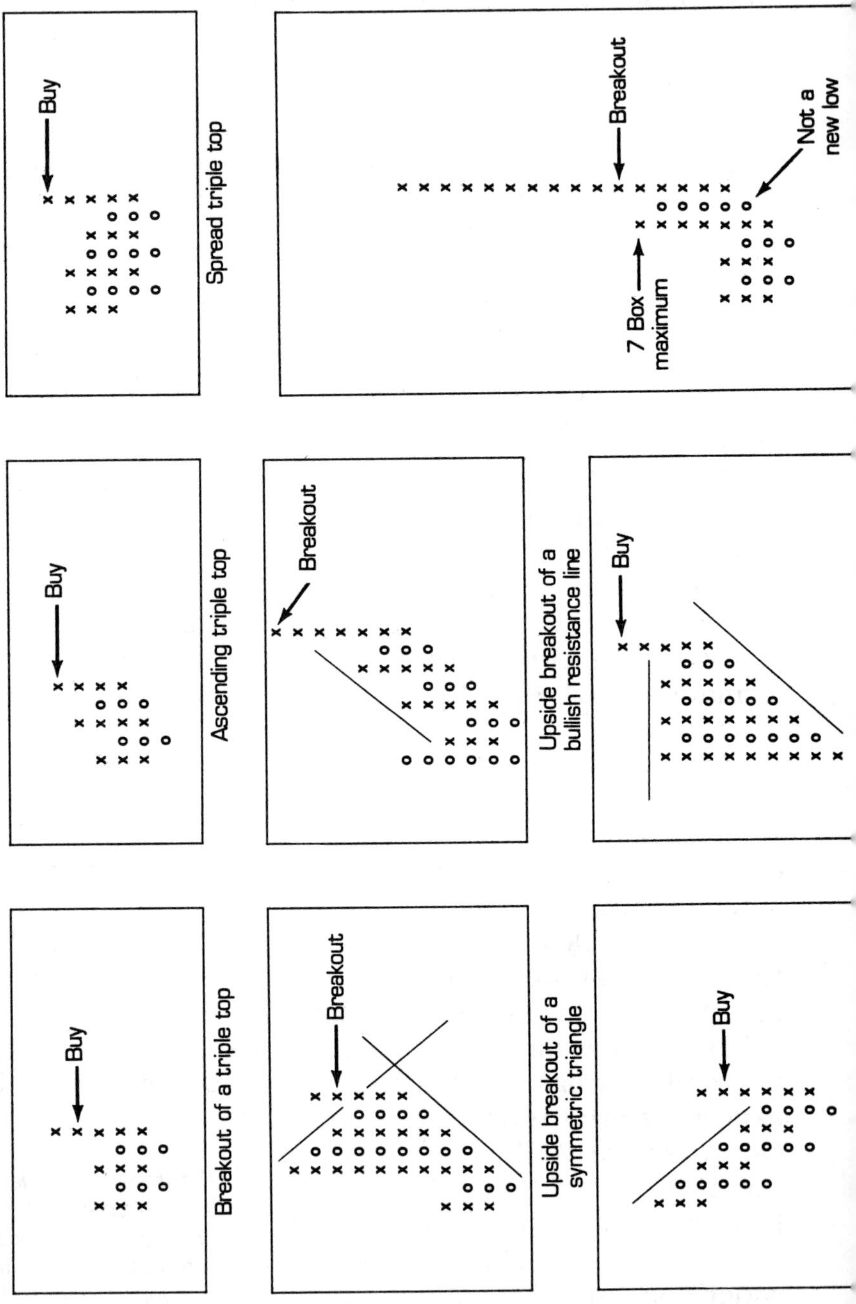

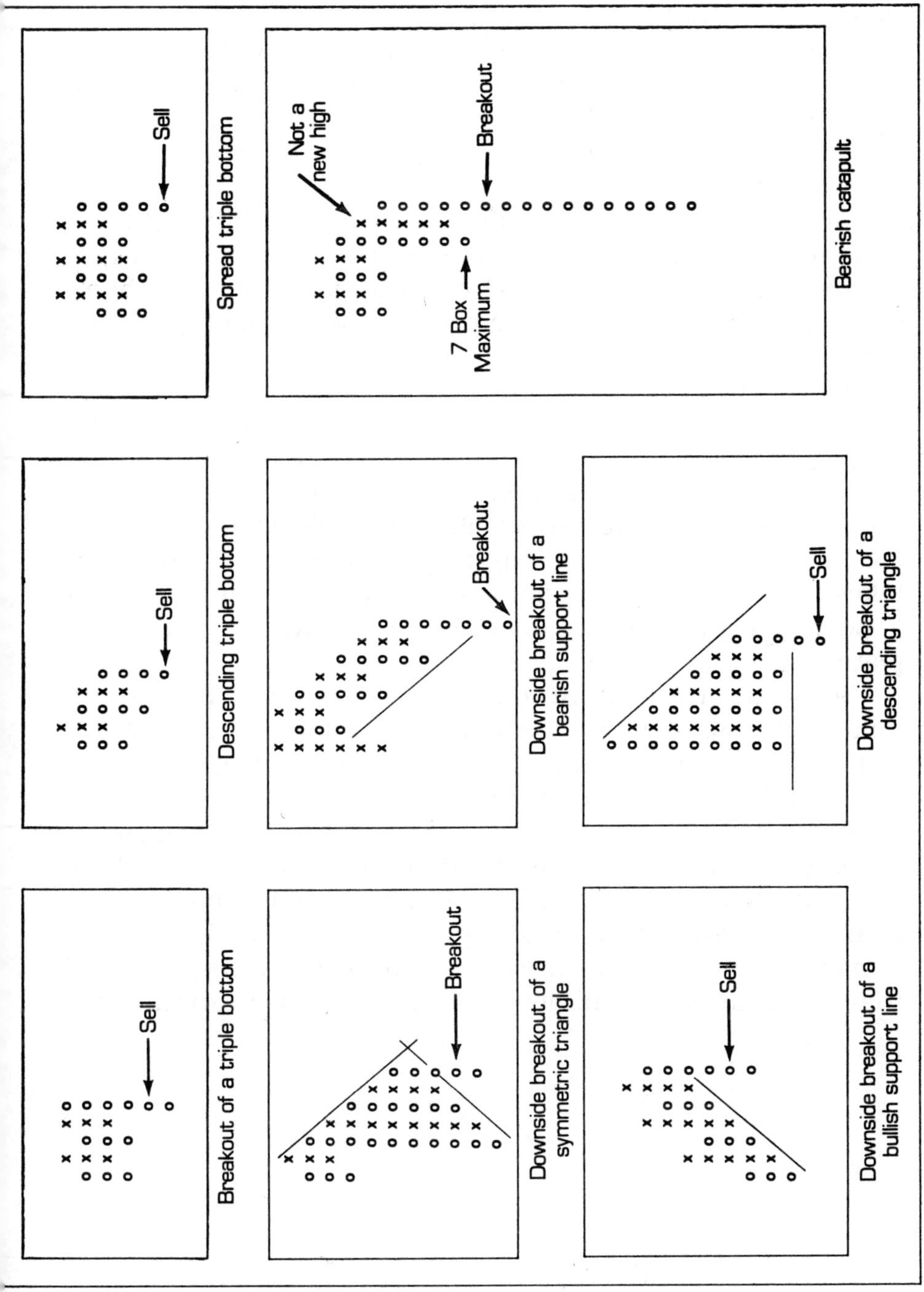
Sell
Spread triple bottom
Not a new high
Breakout
7 Box Maximum
Bearish catapult
Sell
Descending triple bottom
Breakout
Downside breakout of a bearish support line
Sell
Downside breakout of a descending triangle
Sell
Breakout of a triple bottom
Breakout
Downside breakout of a symmetric triangle
Sell
Downside breakout of a bullish support line

evident that would increase our estimate of decline.

This horizontal formation calculation is an obvious advantage in deciding whether the magnitude of a potential price movement is worth your trading time and trouble, as well as anticipating where a stock's next climax or turning point should appear.

Figure charts also make calculating technical strength and weakness easier. With price movements so clearly displayed, it's a simple matter on a figure chart to determine whether a correction or reaction moves a price halfway from its starting point.

Aside from the arithmetic, the general shape of figure charts also spotlights activity that might be clouded by the details of a vertical chart. An upward thrust that breaks the angle of a decline is an eyecatcher on a figure chart. Price oscillations that narrow to a trading range's dead center, the "hinge" of a springboard, are quickly detected on a figure chart. Likewise, an oversold condition shows up on a figure chart as a perpendicular column of prices unbroken by rallies or plateaus.

Seeing a figure chart in action is the best way to understand its usefulness. The hypothetical stock in Figure 6.1 contains a number of clearly defined manipulative movements, with considerable forecasting value.

When you understand what a figure chart is telling you, it becomes a simple matter to integrate it into instances where you think you're getting contradictory signals from the two charts. But with practice and experience, you'll find that these apparent contradictions are simply early warning signals and that one chart's information does not supersede another's.

7
Effective Forecasting

Vertical charts alone are a detailed source of information for the Wyckoff analysis of individual stocks, groups, and the market. But when the analysis combines vertical charts with figure charts, even better results are possible.

Vertical charts (Figure 7.1) with their price-volume information point out where trends are headed, while the price information in figure charts (Figure 7.2) shows just how far the trends should go. The vertical figure chart duo, therefore, makes for more complete diagnosis and more effective forecasts.

Typically, a Wyckoff analyst will be comparing vertical charts of composite averages and group averages, searching for groups that promise to move farther and faster in the same direction as a composite average. A figure chart of a promising group assists in the evaluation by revealing how far a group average should be expected to move.

But even if a group's potential gain isn't enough to get the adrenaline running, there's always the chance that some of its stocks have the wherewithal to move decisively and farther than their average. Typically, the Wyckoff analyst keeps figure

FIGURE 7.1

Vertical (bar) chart of daily high, low and close

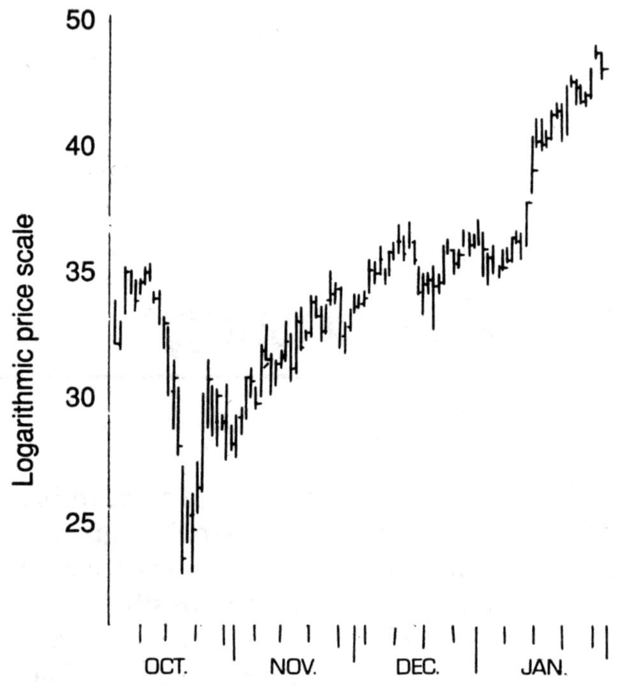

A vertical bar chart plots the day's high, low and close. It can be used for recording the price data of any tradeable.

charts of individual stocks and scans individual volumes in the newspaper each day, on the lookout for volume surges that indicate interest in the stock. In a persistently advancing market, especially, large operators are certain to be searching out laggard stocks and grooming their favorites for distribution to the public. It's these made-to-order opportunities that chart analysis should reveal.

By keeping a backlog of individual price and volume statistics from the newspaper, the analyst can quickly pull together a stock's vertical chart or update an existing one when

FIGURE 7.2

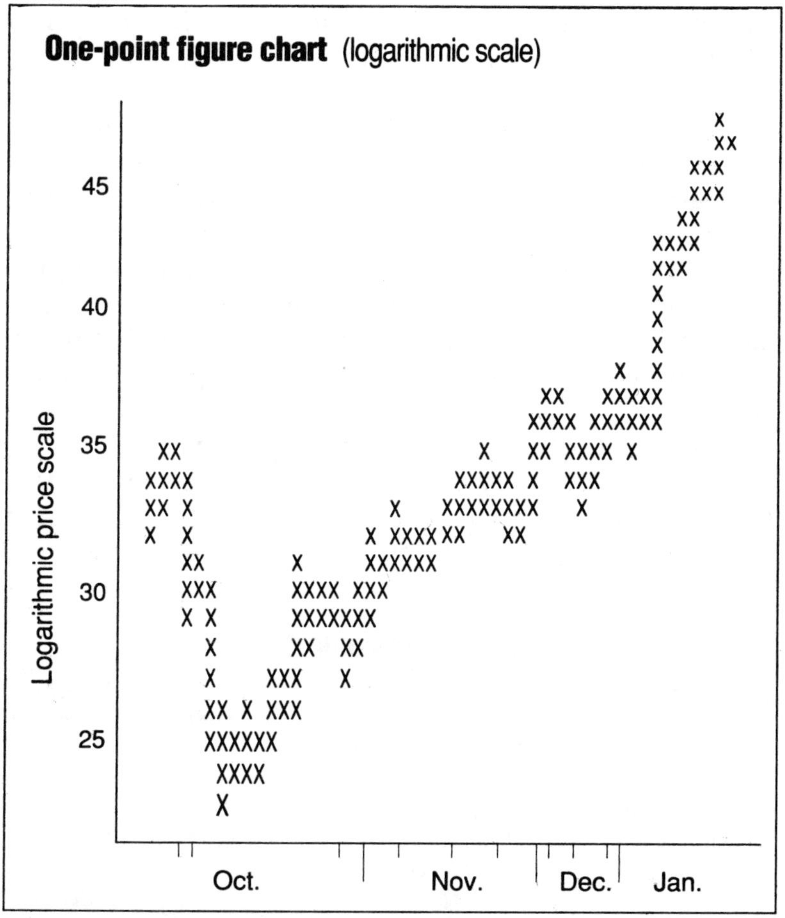

Figure charts are a form of a price filter. Price fluctuations of less than a predetermined amount are ignored. This example does not record any price movements of less than a point.

the figure chart seems to have a strong horizontal base that needs confirmation or denial. The individual vertical chart can then be compared to the group and composite charts.

In this vein, however, it also behooves an analyst to be familiar with a particular stock's history. Unlike averages, individual stocks have personalities all their own. Recognizing their peculiarities will go a long way toward correct chart interpretation. The figure and vertical charts, after all, not only point out the most promising individual stocks in a group, but continue to guide the analyst's timing of trades and placement of stop orders.

Unusual activity is what attracts attention to a particular stock. In a bull market, a stock that shows relatively large volume and small net price change after a number of weeks of dullness would certainly warrant closer inspection. Further signals that a worthwhile advance is in the making include narrow price swings and persistent support at the bottom of a broadening trading zone even in the face of market reactions, small daily volumes, and a time period long enough to tire out weak holders.

At this point, though, it probably wouldn't hurt to wait a bit to make sure the flurry of activity wasn't started by insiders who want to shake off followers and will let the stock react and quiet down again. There is no good financial reason to have

Vertical charts

What is recorded	Deductions therefrom	Indication
Price movement highest, lowest, closing and opening, if desired	Supply and demand Points of resistance and support Marking up and marking down Lines of supply and support Changes of stride and progress of movement Comparative strength and weakness	The TREND, i.e., the direction of the price movement
Volume	Intensity of trading Increasing or diminishing pressure of supply and demand Buying and selling climaxes	WHEN to BUY WHEN to SELL WHEN to CLOSE
Time	Speed of advances and declines Duration of accumulation or distribution	WHERE to place STOP ORDERS
Closing prices	Net gain or loss Changes in pressure up or down	

Figure charts

Price movement	Supply and demand Points of resistance and support Marking up and marking down	The best opportunities
General formations	Accumulation or distribution Lines of supply and support Marking up and marking down	Probable DISTANCE a stock, a group, or a market should move
Horizontal formations	Probable extent of importance of accumulation or distribution	

Wave chart of tape reading

Price movement of the market— Using sensitive leaders as an index	Supply and demand Sentiment of important interests toward the market Critical points of resistance and support Development of accumulation and distribution areas	BEHAVIOR OF the market at critical points in the minor intermediate, and major trends
Volume on alternate buying and selling waves	Changes in pressure up or down Quality and urgency of supply and demand (by comparing volume with activity and time)	
Activity or Intensity of trading	Ability of bull or bear forces to attract following on advances and declines, rallies and reactions	TURNING POINTS in the minor, intermediate and major trends
Time or duration of small buying and selling waves	Speed of advances and declines, rallies and reactions Character of supply and demand whether urgent. leisurely, timid or aggressive	RESPONSIVENESS of the market to buying and selling impulses
Price changes from wave to wave	Net gain or loss Changes in pressure up or down	

trading capital hung up in a stock that may not be ready to move for days or weeks.

If prices fail to move appreciably upward on new rallies, the supply obviously isn't scarce enough to begin an upswing. The vertical chart will tell whether volume increased on the rallies before they were checked and whether price fell back to its previous lows or bullishly set higher supporting points. Without evidence of consistent or sustained demand, however, there would be little hope for a real breakthrough.

Price that bobs up easily on comparatively light volume is a sign that supply is becoming scarce at the low prices. If operators are about to begin their marking-up phase to lock out potential buyers and trap short interests, the stock price should continue to push aggressively past its earlier resistance point or at least not react all the way back to its starting point.

A long order at this point would include a stop close above the resistance point, since a breakout of a long-lived trading range would put the stock on a springboard and the order would still be close to the bottom price of a prolonged rally. However, if price should fall back and confirm that the flurry was simply a buying climax, the trader would still be free to wait for new developments.

An interesting stock in an uninviting group also may demonstrate its potential with a history of refusing to break its supporting points when the market drops. The long horizontal formation this support creates in the figure chart implies a major potential for price appreciation.

The sit-up-and-take-notice signal in this case comes when the stock rallies, dies back, and then the price range narrows to fractions as volume shrinks decidedly. A purchase at this point with a stop placed little more than one point below the support point sets up little chance for damage, should the forecast of an upswing be wrong or premature. In view of the figure chart's wide horizontal formation, the size of the potential move would undoubtedly put the odds in the trader's favor.

A sharp, ensuing price rise and expanding volume would seem to confirm the accuracy of the forecast; a wider price

FIGURE 7.3

One-point figure chart (Arithmetic price scale)

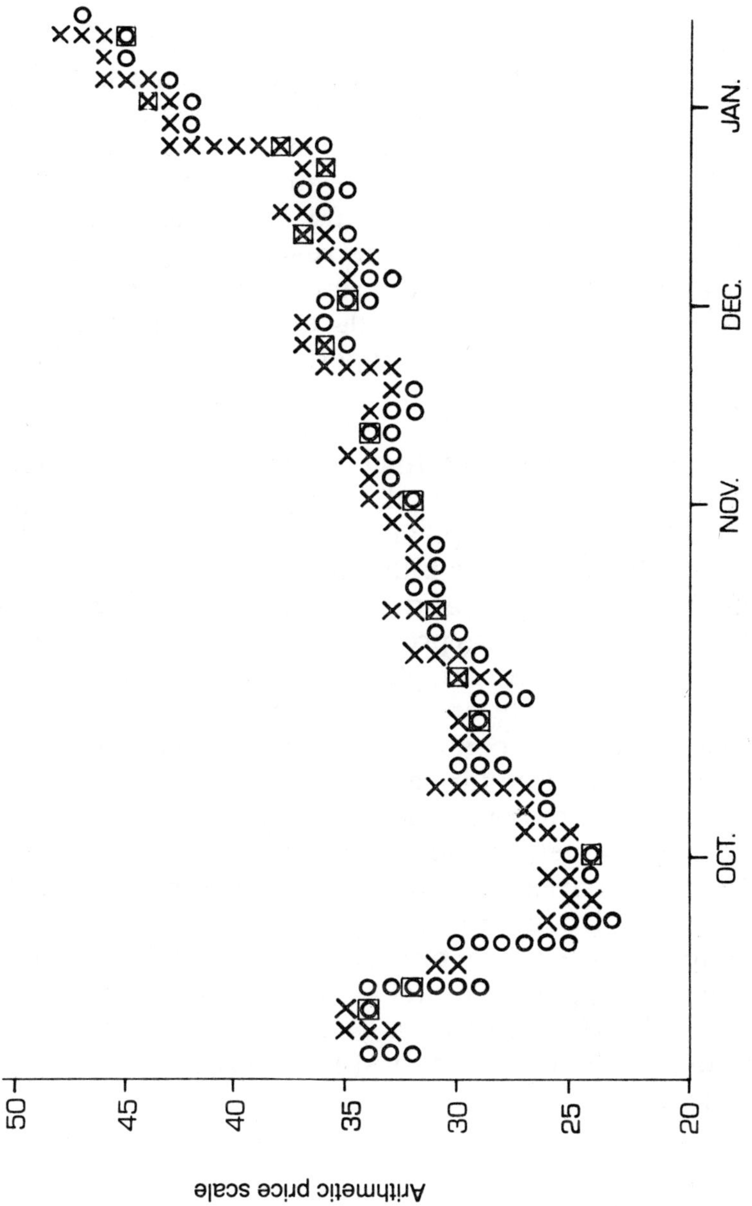

This point & figure chart plots X's for the price advances and O's for the price declines. Any price movement of less than a full point are not recorded.

spread than in previous upthrusts would put price increase in proportion to volume increase and herald the start of a markup. The springboard comes at the advance of the resistance point. At this time, the price range may narrow as volume expands because the stock's operators are absorbing offerings near the resistance point.

This clear indication of the springboard opens up another buying opportunity and would allow the stop to be placed about two points below the resistance point. As the stock advances, the stop would be successively moved a point or so under new supporting levels or under "resting" periods of narrow price range and tapering volume that follow quick upthrusts.

Calculations from the figure chart indicate just how far the rise could go. Nearing this estimate, the analysis looks carefully for signs of a reversal, a bearish turn. When a price near its ultimate target dips and then creeps up slowly with light volume behind it, the indication is that selling pressure has lifted. A succeeding and sudden rush of volume, especially when price is near its previous tops, would cause the Wyckoff analyst to be more suspicious than jubilant. Distribution is probably complete and the next upwave would be the right time to sell out or consider going short, even though the stock hadn't reached its target price.

The wisdom here is not to stick to one indication, such as the price target, to the exclusion of every other factor. Continual comparisons with groups and composite averages put individual stocks into perspective; vertical and figure chart comparisons confirm or deny their separate indications. And when it's apparent a stock isn't going to behave exactly as planned, the smart trader gets out and cuts his or her losses or takes profits that can still be sizable, if not as large as projected.

8
Trendlines: Refinements in Charting

Like any complex activity, chart interpretation needs some aids. Trendlines are one of these aids that help Wyckoff analysts visualize what is occurring in their vertical and figure charts.

The rationale behind trendlines is straightforward. When a stock is being accumulated, it is storing up the force of demand that is the power for an ensuing upward movement. The force of demand gives price a certain momentum to carry it higher until demand is diminished or a new force of supply strong enough to change its path comes into the picture. An indication that demand may be dying out on a rise or that supply is gaining the upper hand is the tendency of prices to arch over or flatten out.

When the growing force of supply overpowers demand, its momentum drives price downward until the force of supply is exhausted or demand is revitalized and brings price to a state of comparative equilibrium. An indication that supply may be dying out on a downswing or that demand is gaining the upper hand is the tendency of prices to round up or level off.

Thus, the momentum that the forces of supply and demand impart to price is as important to a stock market analyst as the momentum imparted to a moving object is to a physicist — and in both cases, momentum can be measured.

In stock analysis, momentum is measured by the angular climb or the downward pitch of the vertical bars on vertical line charts. This is the easiest way to visualize trendlines, which are simply straight lines drawn through the successive tops or bottoms of a price moving through minor, intermediate, and major swings.

Trendlines define the stride of price movement, and direct the analyst's attention to prices that may be changing pace or actually reversing their trend. Basically, any threatened violation of a trendline may be signaling that the force of demand or supply that was in effect is now weakening. The force could change its rate of progress up or down or the trend could be in danger of reversal.

Of course, like any other charting aid, trendlines are valuable when they are used with other indicators to open up as complete a picture of the market as possible. It is self-defeating to exaggerate the importance of trendlines and to use them in a purely mechanical way. Judgment is called for in both plotting and interpreting trendlines.

The significance of trendlines is not just that a line is broken, but how it is broken and the conditions under which it occurs. Interpreting the quality of buying or selling around the violation point determines if the direction of breakthrough will continue or if it is a temporary change. Violations of former tops and bottoms and old levels of support and resistance are equally important, but a trader must be able to deduce if a moving stock or average has hit a resting spell or trading range and is likely to resume its movement with as much or more force than before.

Also, an analyst must be careful not to plot trendlines indiscriminately, especially on every minor move. Plotting trendlines without judgment results in confusion and fallacy. The danger in recklessly drawing trendlines is that every horizontal formation is not necessarily a zone of accumulation or distribution. It may simply be a trading range or a zone of comparative equilibrium where small forces are at work and the minor rallies and reactions will tend to neutralize each other. The key is to analyze horizontal formations to make sure they do signify accumulation or distribution. As we know already, this decisive price movement occurs when forces of supply or demand have built up to such a point that when they become unbalanced their power can sustain a move.

It's always best to first locate trendlines on vertical charts because these charts are most sensitive to price movements and afford the most logical placement of the lines. Then, plot the more important trendlines on the figure charts, where the lines may show developments even more strikingly than on the vertical chart.

Plotting trendlines need not be complicated. There are four basic trendlines — support, supply, oversold position, and overbought positions, as shown in Figure 1.

A support line shows an advancing angle in a bull market by passing through two successive points of support (the lowest points of two successive reactions).

A supply line shows the angle of decline of a bear market by passing through two successive points of resistance (the tops of rallies).

An oversold position line is drawn parallel to the supply line and passes through the first point of support (the lowest point of a reaction) that occurs between the supply line's two successive tops.

An overbought position line is drawn parallel to the support line and passes through the first point of resistance (the top of a rally) that occurs between the support line's successive points of support.

The support and oversold position lines alert a trader to buy or cover, while supply and overbought position lines indicate it's time to sell out or go short.

You can see these trendlines developing very clearly on a vertical chart. Let's say our stock or group has hit one rally. As soon as the vertical chart shows well-defined evidence of a

FIGURE 8.1

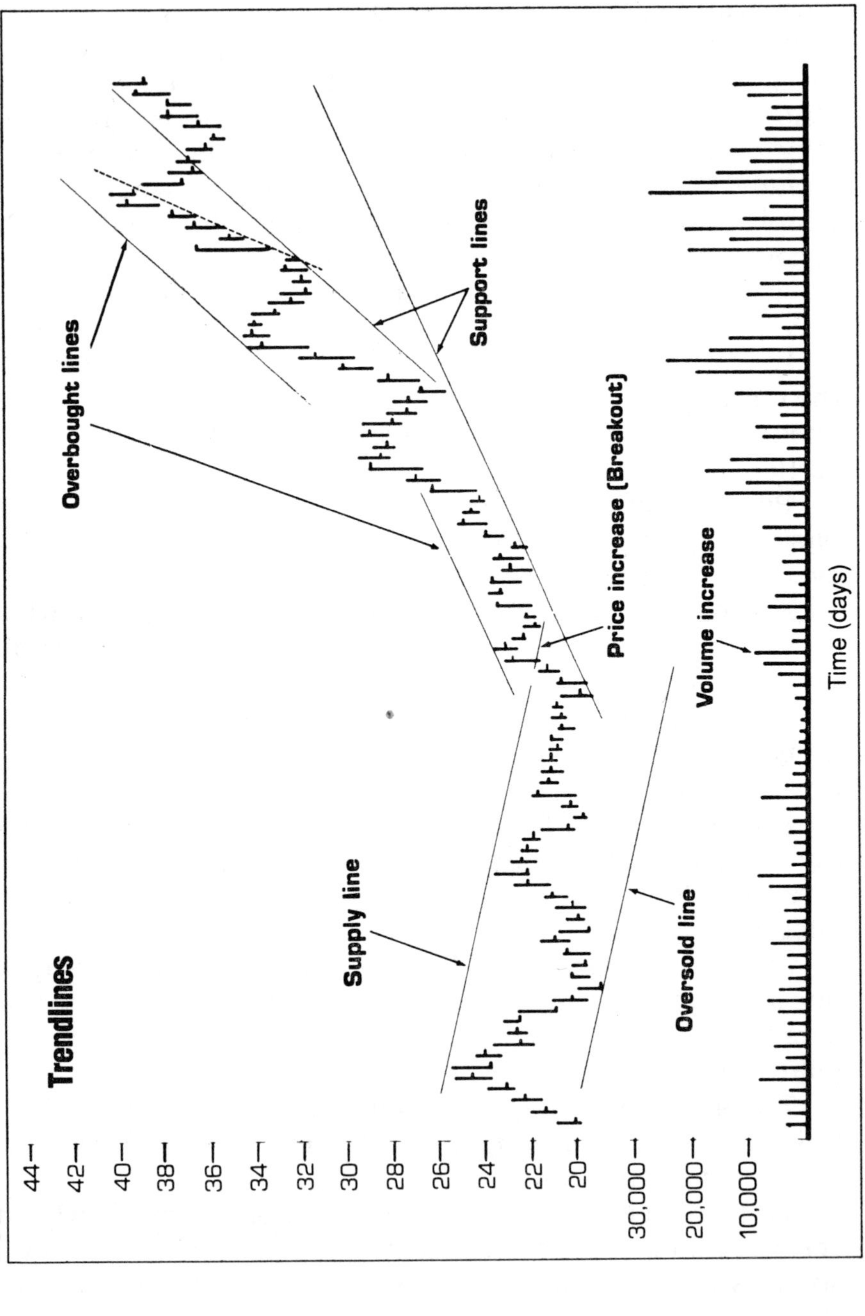
Trendlines
44
42
40
38
36
34
32
30
28
26
24
22
20
30,000
20,000
10,000
Supply line
Oversold line
Overbought lines
Support lines
Price increase (Breakout)
Volume increase
Time (days)

second rally, we can draw a straight line — a supply line — through the two rally tops.

By extending this supply line out to the right, we define the limits that subsequent rallies would be expected to reach until the price develops enough sideways movement, indicating there's enough demand to punch through the supply line.

Should the stock or group break the supply line with increasing volume or a material gain in price — both of which indicate strength — then it's a fairly conclusive indication that the force of demand is being released into a worthwhile upward swing.

Such an advance enables us to plot a support line passing through the low points of two successive reactions. The support line indicates how far future prices should drop on normal, corrective reactions. This, then, gives us an advance hint as to where new demand should kick in if the major upward movement continues.

The continuation of the overall upward movement may very well accelerate as large operators hurry to wind up their campaigns, and another support line at a steeper angle would be warranted. At this point, plotting the support lines of minor movements may help determine if a steep, intermediate advance can continue.

Plotting trendlines on a vertical chart ensures the greatest accuracy in judgment. Transferring the trendlines to one- and three-point figure charts will make trends more noticeable. However, because the figure chart is a condensation of information, indications from its trendlines can contradict those of vertical chart lines. In these cases, the vertical

Figure 8.1
For a declining market, trendlines are drawn along two successive price rallies. The upper channel trendline is called the supply line. At this price level a trader should anticipate supply entering the market if the downtrend continues. The lower channel trendline is called the oversold line. At this price level a trader should expect that selling is unlikely to occur at any lower prices. During an advancing market, the upper channel trendline is the overbought line. Prices should falter at these price levels due to a lack of new buyers. The lines of the lower side of the upward channel are called support lines. Buyers should be moving back into the market at these price levels.

FIGURE 8.2

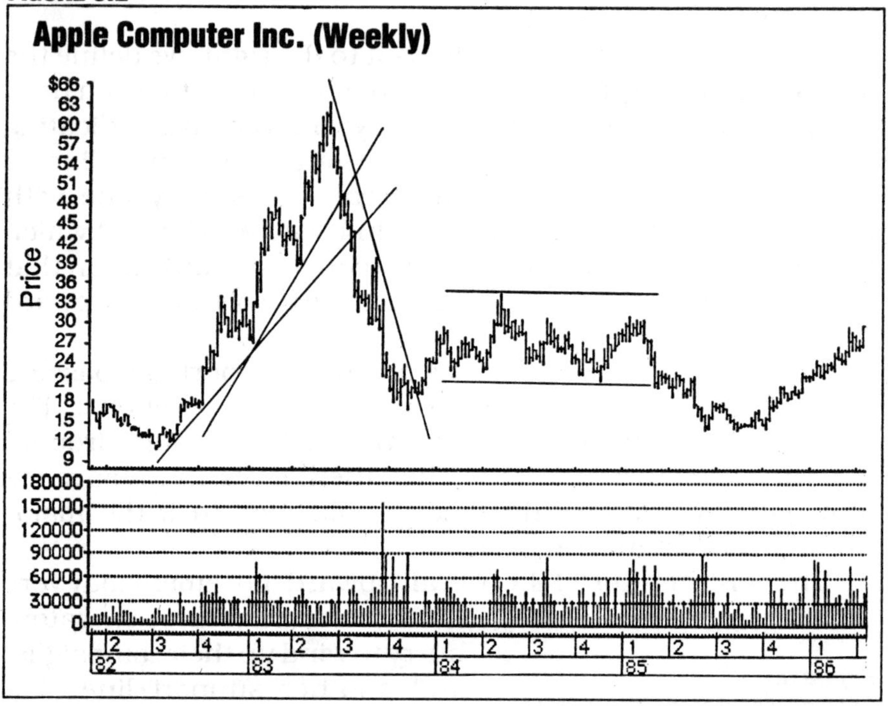

Apple Computer during 1982 through early 1986 had uptrends, downtrends and sideways trends. Even without trendlines drawn, these trends are readily apparent.

chart is the one to follow.

We can see how vertical and figure chart trendlines are related in Figure 8.1. Here, we're looking back at a stock or group in decline. An initial supply line drawn through two rally tops and extended to the right shows how far a rally would have to jump to signal a trend change.

Should the rate of decline accelerate, a new and steeper supply line is warranted. A supply line pitched almost perpendicularly to the x-axis points to an emerging oversold position. When this steeper supply line is breached by a vigorous rally it indicates that demand is overcoming supply. We anticipate that this selling climax will be followed by a technical rally.

If the technical rally does not break through the original supply line, it's a sign that the rally is ending. The net normal

FIGURE 8.3

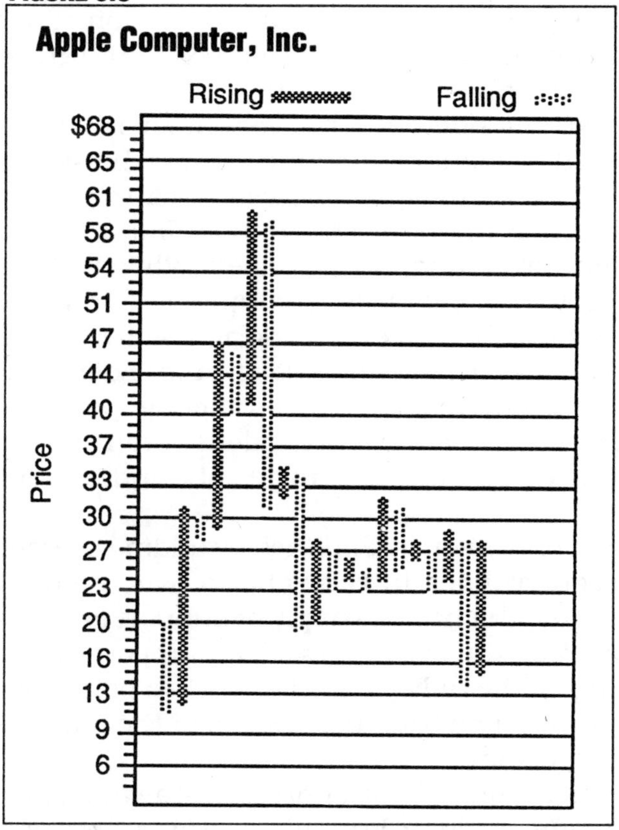

Example of a three-point figure chart with a $1.00 box size and a $3.00 box reversal for Apple Computer, Inc., weekly prices. Note that figure charts use no time scale.

event would be a secondary reaction to test support. At this point, our one-point figure chart would tell us just how high a recovery could rise. A quick look at the vertical chart tells us whether the potential rise would break the vertical chart supply line. When the rally breaks the line, it's a confirmation that the trend is changing from technical weakness to technical strength.

At times, trendlines do not give clear-cut indications, making it all the more important to continue drawing on complete chart analyses. For example, when the reaction to our trend-changing rally breaks an existing support line, is it a sign of further weakness and a resumption of decline, or is it a temporary and minor selling climax? Only further developments will clear up the question.

The ensuring sideways price movement marks the reaction as just another point at which to redraw the support line. As the price swings to dead center, we also can draw a new supply line and notice that the new supply line and the redrawn support line cross and form an apex. While Wyckoff analysts eschew geometric patterns, the apex is one formation that highlights how the price is working itself to a springboard, poised to release the accumulating force of demand. The apex shows up even more strikingly on the one-point figure chart. A three-point figure chart will condense even more history into a small space and bring the angles of trendlines into sharper focus.

You can refine your trendlines by adding oversold position and overbought lines to your charts, where possible. To do this, you must first have a supply or support line. Where a rally occurs between the two points of the support line, draw a line from the top of the rally parallel to the two points of the supply line and draw a line from the bottom of the reactions parallel to the supply line.

If the price tends to stop short or pull away from an oversold or overbought position line, it's a strong hint of impending change of pace or change of trend.

Of course, any trendline must be judged in light of all other technical factors. It is best to think of trendlines as hints rather than positive indications.

9

Selecting the Best Individual Stocks

Our discussion of Wyckoff's analytical methods has so far concentrated on deductive reasoning to reach investment or trading conclusions. We first determined the position and trend of the general market, then the positions and trend of group averages, and finally selected individual stocks based on their ability to move in harmony with those larger trends.

The opposite approach — inductive reasoning — offers the experienced Wyckoff analyst a valuable way to double-check those conclusions. I emphasize "experienced analyst" because determining the positions of individual stocks first and then proceeding to the market and groups requires more skill and judgment, as well as more time for analysis.

To make inductive reasoning easier and to help the deductive analyst make better individual stock selections, Wyckoff devised a recordkeeping device in 1916 called a position sheet. A position sheet simply keeps track of the potential movements of individual stocks. This helps the Wyckoff analyst determine which stocks offer the best trading opportunities, judge stocks' turning points, determine group trends, forecast group movements, and ascertain the trend of the entire market.

The premise behind the position sheet is straightforward. Every stock is either bullish, bearish or neutral; in harmony or out of harmony with the general market's trend. The position sheet tracks individual stocks according to five possible positions that Wyckoff identifies as:

Position 1 — A rally or minor move up without material reaction; the stock should indicate a short upward swing of roughly 10-15% of its present market price.

Position 2 — An advance without material reaction; the stock should be ready for a long upward swing that, in points, amounts to more than 10-15% of its current market price.

Position 3 — A reaction without any material rally; the stock should indicate a short downward swing, a drop equivalent to 10-15% of present market price.

Position 4 — A decline without any material rally; the stock should indicate a long downward swing amounting to more than 10-15% of current market price.

Position 5 — Neutral; no definite indication of a move in either direction.

Knowing these positions for a number of stocks, the Wyckoff analyst can make decisions about the market and groups and, therefore, use that information to select individual stocks able to move quickly and surely in the forefront of the market.

Positions 2 and 4, the heralds of advance and decline, are the most important to a Wyckoff trader because they are the positions in which the most money can be made. These stocks promise such sufficiently large swings that it's realistic to expect that an intermediate swing is in the works, amounting to 10, 20, or 30 points.

Positions 1 and 3, the rally and reaction, are less important but do tell the Wyckoff trader when to buy or sell to advantage — that is, the tops of rallies. These indications of short moves in the neighborhood of three to five or eight points for a moderately priced stock help Wyckoff analysts select the right time to take their trading positions.

Constructing a position sheet starts with a list of individual stocks — at least 50 but preferably 100 or more — arranged according to groups (Figure 9.1). To the left of the stock names are two columns, one for Position 1 and one for Position 2. To the right of the stock names are two more columns for Positions 3 and 4. Space is reserved in the lower right-hand corner of the page to tally the number of stocks in each position, to note the overall market's position and the analyst's trading position.

Although you can learn to keep a position sheet with only 20 stocks, in actual market operations Wyckoff recommends covering 50 to 100 or more — roughly an hour's work each day.

The daily position sheet begins with the analysis of figure and vertical charts of individual stocks to observe their technical positions. Preliminary decisions about Positions 2 and 4, the advance and decline, can be made from figure charts and the conclusions checked with the aid of vertical charts. Vertical charts are indispensable in determining Positions 1 and 3, the rally and reaction, because volume is the best means of judging the turning points of these minor swings.

For efficiency, Wyckoff recommends following stock movements with figure charts, and when a stock shows itself working into a promising position, making up its vertical chart to observe its behavior in detail to apply all the factors needed for complete analysis.

A stock can show its ability to develop a Position 1 minor upward move: 1) in the nature of its rally from a low point, 2) at a level where the minor move is the forerunner of a large advance, or 3) at a level in a

***Figure 9.1** (see next page) A position sheet tracks individual stocks according to five possible positions. Position 1: The stock indicates a short upward swing of roughly 10-15% is due. Position 2: The stock indicates a material advance of more than 10-15% is due. Position 3: The stock indicates a short downward swing of 10-15% is due. Position 4: The stock indicates a downward swing of more than 10-15% is due. Position 5: A neutral outlook is warranted regarding the stock.*

FIGURE 9.1

Position sheet

1	2	Stock	3	4
		Aerospace		
X		BA		
X	X	GD		
		LK	X	X
		MD		
X	X	NOC		
X		RTN		
		UTX	X	X
		Airlines		
		AMR	X	X
		DAL	X	X
		EAF	X	X
		FDX	X	
		NWA	X	
		LUV		
X	X	UAL		
		Amusements		
	X	DIS	X	
X		MCA		
		Auto		
X		C		
X		F		
X		GM		
		Banking		
		BAC	X	
		CMB	X	X

1	2	Stock	3	4
		Cosmetics		
	X	AVP	X	
X	X	GS		
		REV		
		Diversified		
	X	AXP	X	
		AVT		
		DKI	X	
X	X	FLR		
X	X	GW		
		ITT	X	
X	X	LIT		
	X	LTR	X	
	X	PC	X	
X	X	WCI		
X	X	WMB		
		TW		
		Drugs		
		ABT	X	
X	X	AHP		
		BMY	X	
	X	LLY	X	
X	X	MRK		
	X	PFE	X	
X	X	SQB		
X	X	SYN		
		UPJ		

1	2	Stock	3	4
		Medical		
		BDX	X	X
		BAX	X	
		HCA	X	
		HUM		
X	X	JNJ		
	X	MDT		
		Metals		
X		AA		
X		AMX		
X		N		
		NL	X	
		PD	X	X
		RLM	X	X
		Metals-Gold/Silver		
		ASA		
X	X	CRK		
X	X	DM		
	X	HM	X	
X	X	HL		
		Office Equipment		
		BGH		
		DBD	X	X
	X	MMM	X	
X	X	NCR		
		XRX		

1	2	Stock	3	4
		Rail Equipment		
		GMT	X	
		Rail Shipping		
X	X	BNI		
X	X	UNP		
		Retailing		
		JCP		
		KM		
X		RDS	X	
		S	X	X
X		TAN		
		WMT		
		Soft Drinks		
X		KO		
X	X	PEP		
		Steel/Coal		
		BS	X	X
		X		
		Telephone		
X	X	T		
X		CQ		
		WU	X	X
		AIT	X	X
		GTE	X	X

1	2	Stock	3	4
X	X	JWC		
		LPX	X	
		ML		
		OCF	X	
		WY	X	
		Brokerage Firms		
	X	EFH	X	
	X	MER	X	
X	X	PSB		
		PWJ		
		Chemicals		
		ACY		
X		BIG		
	X	DIA	X	
		DOW	X	
	X	DD		
X	X	EY		
X	X	IGL		
X	X	LZ		
	X	MTC	X	
	X	PG	X	
X	X	UK		
		Computers		
X		CDA		
X		CBU		
X		CVN		
		CYR	X	
X		DGN		
X	X	AUD		
		DEC	X	
X	X	HON		
		IBM		
		SY	X	X
24	21	**Total**	24	8

1	2	Stock	3	4
	X	RCA	X	
		TEK	X	
	X	TRW	X	
X		TDY		
X		WX		
		Electronics/Semiconductor		
		AMD		
		MOT	X	
		NSM	X	
X	X	TXN		
X	X	UTR		
		Food		
		GIS		
		SA		
X		RAL		X
		PSY	X	X
		Hotels		
X		HIA		
		HLT		
		Insurance		
X		AET		
X	X	FG		
		LNC	X	X
		MMC		
X	X	TIC		
		Machinery		
X		CAT		
		CKL	X	X
X		CSP		
		DE	X	X
		DI	X	X
		IR	X	X
21	21	**Total**	19	3

1	2	Stock	3	4
X	X	LLX		
	X	MOB	X	
	X	OXY	X	
X	X	PZL		
X	X	RD		
		SNT		
		TX		
		Oil Exploration		
X	X	BKO		
		HT	X	
	X	HAL	X	
X	X	MSA		
	X	MDR	X	
X	X	SLB		
		Paper		
X	X	CHA		
		ZB	X	
		KMB	X	
		IP		
		Photo/Optical		
		BOL	X	
X		EK		
X		PRD		
		Publishing		
	X	GCI	X	
		MHP	X	
	X	TL	X	
X		DND		
		Radio & TV		
X		CCB		
		CBS		
		TFB	X	
21	22	**Total**	24	8

1	2	Stock	3	4
		No Group		
X	X	BLY		
	X	CLO	X	
X		ETN		
X		MDA		
X		MCD		
X		TOY		
15	8	**Totals**	15	6

1	2	**Summary**	3	4
24	21	Col. 1	24	8
21	21	Col. 2	19	3
21	23	Col. 3	24	8
15	8	Col. 4	15	6
81	72	**Totals**	82	25

Trend Summary

1	2	**Indicates**	3	4
	X	Averages	X	
X		Summary	X	

Position should be:

Long ~~Short~~ ~~Neutral~~

Date: May 1 Hr.:3 p.m.

trading range that indicates a small move through the previous top of the range.

To get into Position 2, the stock may show its promise of a large advance with: 1) evidence of accumulation at the bottom of a downward movement, 2) in a resting period that follows a previous advance where there was evidence of absorption (reaccumulation) in preparation for further advance, and/or 3) its ability to persistently advance through a series of higher tops and bottoms on successive minor moves — even though there was no evidence of previous preparation for the advance.

The small downward move of Position 3 may herald itself: 1) in the nature of a stock's reaction from a high point, 2) at a level where the reaction is the forerunner of a large decline, or 3) at a level in a trading range where the stock cannot rally and will probably drop through the previous support level.

A stock indicates its potential for the large decline of Position 4 when it: 1) shows evidence of being under distribution at the top of an advance; 2) is in a period of rest after a previous decline where it gives evidence of meeting new supply (redistribution) in preparation for a further decline; or 3) is at a level in a trading range where the stock persistently declines through a series of lower bottoms and tops on successive minor moves — even though there was no clear-cut evidence of distribution in preparation for the decline.

The Neutral Position is equally important, since trading when indications are not clear is an invitation to losses. A stock is in a Neutral Position when there is no definite movement in either direction or there's doubt as to its ability to move decisively. This occurs when: 1) a stock gives tentative but unconvincing indications that it will rally or react further; 2) a stock hesitates during an advance or decline without convincing indication of a change of trend; 3) the indications of a stock's price and volume indications are contradicory or inconclusive; or 4) when a stock's price is extremely dull in a narrow trading range or swings up and down without developing any well-defined trend.

The Wyckoff analyst determining the technical position of each stock places a pencil mark on the Position Sheet in the appropriate position column. Pencil, rather than pen, is recommended so the Position Sheet can be reused for the next day's decisions, something we'll touch on in a moment.

Once the day's analysis is complete and the Position Sheet filled, the next step is to determine the trend of the general market. It's simply a matter of totaling the number of stocks judged to be in each position, and comparing the number in the very bullish Position 2 and to the total number judged to be in the very bearish Position 4. The ratio of bull to bear stocks indicates in which of the five positions the overall market sits. For example, if 40 stocks indicate they are in Position 2, and 10 are in Position 4, the market is obviously leaning to the bullish Position 2.

Although this analysis concentrates on Positions 2 and 4, stocks can be simultaneously in two positions. A combination of Positions 3 and 2 indicates a short move down before a long move up; Positions 1 and 4 indicate a short move up before a long move down. The only contradictory combinations would be Positions 2 and 4 — an advance and a decline — and Positions 1 and 3 — a rally and reaction.

One position also can build into another — Position 1, the rally, can build into Position 2, the advance, but the reverse is not true. Likewise, Position 3 can build into Position 4, but not vice versa. So while a stock can change between Positions 2 and 4, these positions should not be reduced either to Position 1 or 3.

As a double check of your conclusion about the market's position from the position sheet, compare it to an independent conclusion drawn from the trend chart of group averages. It's very unlikely that an out-and-out contradiction between the position sheet and trend chart would actually occur in the market, so if it shows up, it's time to rethink some deductions.

The same procedure of totaling the number of stocks in each position and comparing the totals leads to the next step of determining which groups on the position sheet offer the best trading or investment opportunities. By comparing each group's position to the overall market position, a Wyckoff analyst finds the groups most closely aligned with the large-

FIGURE 9.2

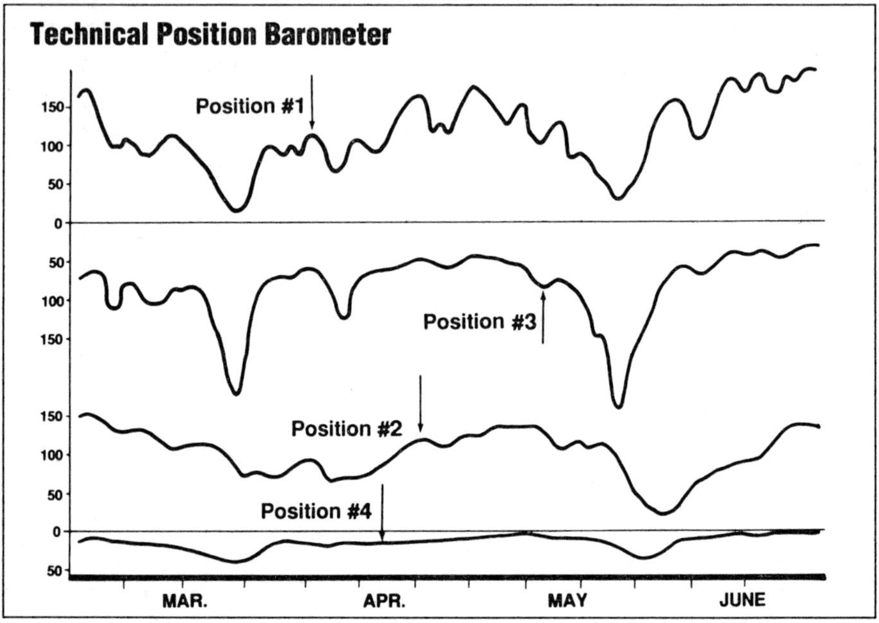

The technical barometer is the daily plotting of the total number of stocks in each position. The number of stocks in each position can provide significant information regarding the growing weakness or strength of the stock market.

scale trend and most likely to contain stocks able to move first, fastest, and farthest with the market.

In finally selecting individual stocks from the position sheet, the analyst again looks for the strongest positions in harmony with the market. Further research compares these stocks against each other, with the trend chart, and with the vertical chart of group averages. The timing of actual purchases is guided by the technical position of the stock as shown on its individual vertical chart.

Maintaining a position sheet can be a valuable aid to judgment. Wyckoff recommends that it be constructed daily. If all position marks are made with pencil, one sheet can be reused for quite some time. A permanent summary of each day's work can then be charted on a Technical Position Barometer (Figure 9.2), a chart that becomes a valuable trend forecaster.

Constructing the Technical Position Barometer is a quick task, requiring no more than a day-by-day plotting of the total number of stocks in each position. Each position is a separate line on the graph. The barometer shows at a glance whether the number of stocks in certain positions are gradually increasing or decreasing. This becomes a significant clue to the growing strength or weakness of the market's technical position.

To conclude this discussion of the position sheet, we can see how Wyckoff himself would judge the technical positions of an individual stock from its vertical or figure chart movements. At the beginning of the analysis, the price of Stock ABC has been hovering between 30 and 34 for two weeks with no sign of definite movement. It is in the Neutral Position.

When the price rises steadily for four successive days and the volume on the fourth day markedly increases, it suggests a buying climax. The fifth day's price hits a fractionally higher top of 35 5/8, then closes near the low. The stock is due for a reaction and is moved tentatively to Position 3. It is a tentative move because there are not sufficient data to determine just how far it might react. A one-point figure chart should give an indication of the amount of reaction; a definite Position 3 would be given when it's clear that the reaction would bring at least a 10% drop in price.

In this case, Stock ABC reacts normally and its price drops to 32, not quite a 10% drop. But instead of rallying, the stock price goes into a narrow range with shrinking volume and works itself into an apex or dead center — definitely a sign of a Position 3.

The stock price continues to plummet toward a previous support level. The steepness of the drop creates the possibility of an oversold position, and a sharp volume increase on the decline suggests a minor selling climax. Continuing heavy volume and shortened downward price thrust in the next days indicate that demand is overcoming supply and the reaction has achieved the objective forecast by the figure chart.

When the stock price moves laterally in a narrow range near a previous support level and with low volume for two more sessions, the position is moved to Neutral. The stock is too finely balanced between bearish and bullish forces to make a definite decision. The next days' actions must first be scrutinized.

A technical rally breaks a minor trend supply line and volume is relatively large. The rally continues a second day and is close to the objective indicated by the figure chart, but a volume surge warns to be on the lookout for another change. A quick reaction on the third day cancels the rise; the price hangs near former lows, but volume is not much reduced. Several more days of sideways price movement at constant volume and lows that tend to edge upward looks like good buying rather than good selling, and the stock goes into Position 1.

The stock won't move into Position 2 until there are additional indications that the campaign of accumulation has been completed and the groundwork for a significant advance is being laid. Until then, the stock may bounce from Position 1 to Neutral and perhaps even back to Position 3.

In this case, Position 2 comes about after two weeks of dull sagging price movement exhausts itself in a quick dip to the supporting level without bringing out any quantity of offerings. By now, the figure chart promises a rise of more than 20 points, and the springboard points directly at Position 2 and the time to buy.

Judging technical positions is a matter of practice and experience. Sitting down with historical vertical and figure charts will help to develop skill in determining positions. From there, apply your know-how to charts constructed in real time, from day to day, and put yourself to the test in paper trading.

10
Refining Chart Analysis

At this point in our examination of Wyckoff's methodology for stock market analysis, we have explored all the major tenets of his classic technique — from basic charting to the more esoteric consideration of trendlines, position sheets, and chart interaction. Now we are ready to pursue the technical refinements that distinguish slapdash amateurs from proficient and effective traders and investors.

If this is your beginning foray into technical analysis, you may be feeling a bit overwhelmed by all that we've introduced about the Wyckoff method. At this point, too, experienced technical traders may have the natural reaction to pick and choose pieces of Wyckoff's design and try to meld them with other, more familiar systems. To both the new student and the proficient analyst I would caution against "any inclination to grow faint-hearted," as Wyckoff would put it, and to take shortcuts with his method. The Wyckoff method is a complete system, combining mental attitude with interconnected technical details. Separating some facets of this method from the rest is like drawing random pieces from a puzzle box — you've got the parts, but no picture.

If the Wyckoff method at this point in your study seems unduly complex, rest assured that with practice it will all boil down to a matter of routine reasoning. Steps that may seem detailed at first become second nature. Principles that appear numerous and confounding soon become instinct.

I have summarized Wyckoff's most important tests for buying and selling in Figure 1. The indications are applicable to market and group averages, as well as individual stocks. Notice, too, that these telltale tests rely on both figure and vertical charts, the two charts from which all refinements are created and the two charts that are always used in conjunction with one another to portray the most accurate picture of market activity.

Before we look for these indications on sample figure and vertical charts, the Wyckoff student should incorporate a few more market phenomena into his or her body of knowledge. These can occur at various times and, unless understood, can lead to erroneous conclusions from the vertical and figure charts.

The first of these phenomena is the shakeout — either ordinary or terminal. An ordinary shakeout is a sharp downward movement such as an exaggerated selling climax. A terminal shakeout is even more pronounced. It is a rapid downward movement occurring at or near the end of extensive preparation for an advance.

Viewing it through the eyes of a market "manipulator," the plunge of a terminal shakeout is intended to scare a stock's persistent hangers-on into selling out, to catch stop orders placed below earlier support prices, or even induce the unwary public into short selling. The manipulator buys up the stock offered by sellers frightened or caught by the terminal shakeout, and the ensuing scarcity of the stock on the market sends the price rapidly or gradually higher.

A thrust is the reverse of a shakeout. It may also by known as an upthrust or a terminal markup. Whatever the name, it is a sharp runup and out of an area of distribution, or a temporary bulge through the top of a trading range. The inability to hold these thrusts or quick bulges indicates

FIGURE 10.1

Buying and Selling Tests

BUYING TESTS (Applied to an average or a stock after a decline)

Indication:	Determined From:
1) Downside objective accomplished	Figure Chart
2) Activity bullish (volume increases on rallies and decreases on reactions)	Vertical Chart
3) Preliminary support	Vertical and Figure
4) Average or stock stronger than market (i.e., more responsive on rallies and more resistant to reactions)	Vertical Chart
5) Downward stride broken (i.e., supply line penetrated)	Vertical or Figure
6) Higher supports (daily low)	Vertical or Figure
7) Higher tops (daily high prices rising)	Vertical or Figure
8) Base forming (horizontal price line)	Figure Chart
9) Estimated profit is at least three times the indicated risk Vertical Chart for stop order placement	Figure Chart for profit objective

SELLING TESTS (Applied to an average or a stock after an advance)

Indication:	Determined From:
1) Upside objective accomplished	Figure Chart
2) Activity bearish (volume decreases on rallies and increases on reactions)	Vertical Chart
3) Preliminary support	Vertical and Figure
4) Average or stock weaker than market (i.e., more responsive on reactions and sluggish on rallies)	Vertical Chart
5) Upward stride broken (i.e., support line penetrated)	Vertical or Figure
6) Lower tops (daily high prices falling)	Vertical or Figure
7) Lower supports (daily low prices falling)	Vertical or Figure
8) Crown forming (lateral movement)	Figure Chart
9) Estimated profit is at least three times the indicated risk Vertical Chart for stop order placement	Figure Chart for profit objective

weakness.

At times, the trader may also be caught unawares by another phenomenon — a sharp rally out of a plunging oversold condition that is not heralded by the customary evidence of accumulation. In such a case, a declining stock's figure chart may not show the usual long, compact horizontal trading range that forecasts a major recovery. Instead, the horizontal trading range indicates a small upward movement. The attuned Wyckoff analyst, however, notices that this small upward movement would break the diagonal trendline formed by the previous decline. With such a possibility, the entire downward movement could be re-evaluated as a probable zone of support and previous horizontal formations reviewed for the potential price objective of a major upswing.

Of course, a figure chart's horizontal formations alone cannot be taken as evidence of an impending rally. A "chart fiend," as Wyckoff calls them, might easily mistake a figure chart's long horizontal formation as the basis for a tremendous rise when, in fact, the vertical chart would plainly show it to be an extended trading range where small changes in supply and demand neutralized each other for a considerable time.

As a quick review, we'll examine the vertical and figure charts of a hypothetical stock (Figure 2) for buying tests and other phenomena. The following numbered comments correspond to the charts that depict the stock of Hypothetical, Inc., recovering from an oversold position.

1) The speed and severity of the decline from 31-1/2 to 17-7/8 occurs without corrective rallies and creates an oversold condition.

2) During the decline, the sudden breaking of previous supports around 24-25 appears to be a shakeout and is confirmed with the rapid recovery revealed by the three-point figure chart.

3) An abnormal volume expansion indicates the movement's climax and the development of preliminary support (Buying Test No. 3).

4) The line of 29s in the one-point figure chart indicates a downside objective, which is accomplished when the stock reaches 18 (Buying Test No. 1).

   Steps 1 through 4 are the preliminary symptoms of a turning point. Here, the stock would be placed tentatively on the position sheet in Position 1, and a purchase somewhere around the low point, say, 19 with a stop at 16-5/8, could be ventured.

5) A quick rally to 20-3/8 with light volume indicates a scarcity of offerings, and breaking the supply line B-C confirms the change from weakness to strength (Buying Test No. 5).

6) The one-point figure chart more clearly defines the preliminary support. When the price reacts from 20-3/8 to 18-5/8 on light volume, it is definitely in Position 1 on the position sheet and it is time to buy another lot or make the first purchase if the earlier opportunity was missed.

7) A fast rally on increasing, but still light volume, adds to the accumulating evidence of strength (Buying Test No. 2), and the stock is clearly stronger than the market that is hitting new lows.

8) The rally is checked by general market weakness and the supply line A-B. Cancel Position 1 in anticipation of a setback and wait for another buying opportunity if it reacts toward the 18 supports on diminishing volume.

   When the stock reacts, volume tapers off, and the price holds at higher supports, it is back in Position 1. On the figure chart, support at at 19 has stretched to a count of five, and the line of 20s is at six.

9) Price and volume have narrowed to an extreme, developing a perfect apex, or hinge. A rally now would easily penetrate the supply line A-B and put the stock on the springboard at 21 — another buying opportunity.

10) Price penetrates the supply line A-B on light volume (a bullish sign) and responds to an upturn in the general market. With higher supports and higher tops, it fulfills

FIGURE 10.2

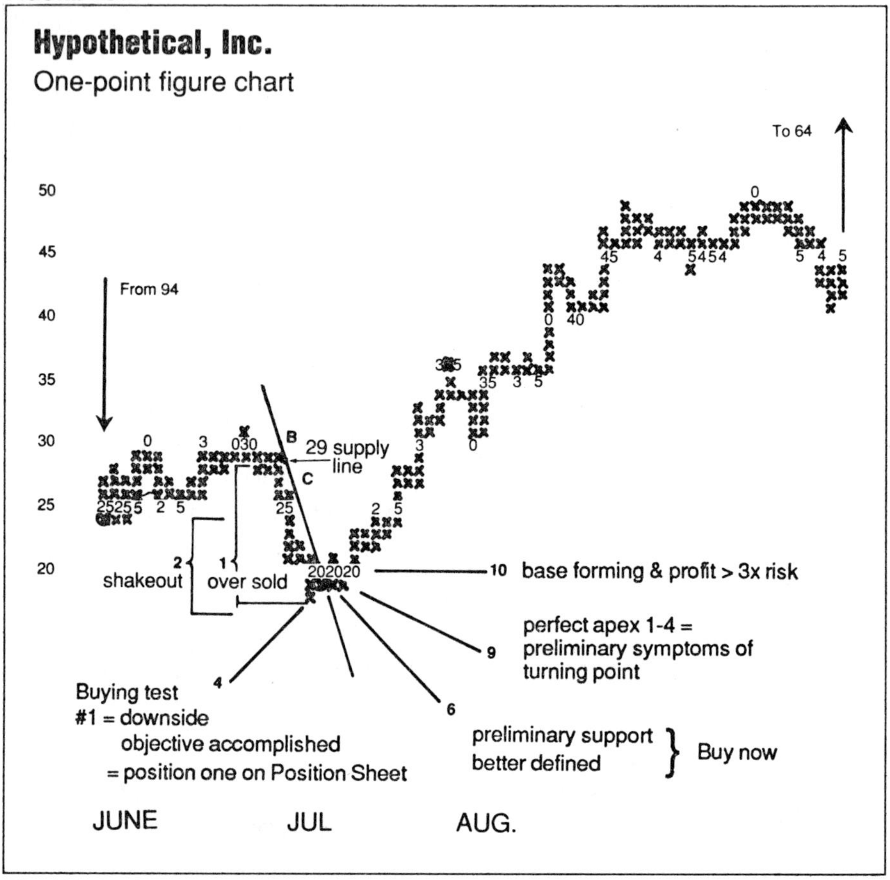

The Wyckoff method applies step-by-step procedures for decision making.

Buying Tests No. 6 and 7. The stock is now in Position 2 and the figure chart adds one more point to the objective, fulfilling Buying Tests No. 8 and 9.

With this example and the consolidated lists of buying and selling tests, take the time to review the charts pictured in previous chapters and other historical charts. When you can recognize buying and selling tests with an entire chart in front

FIGURE 10.2 (continued)

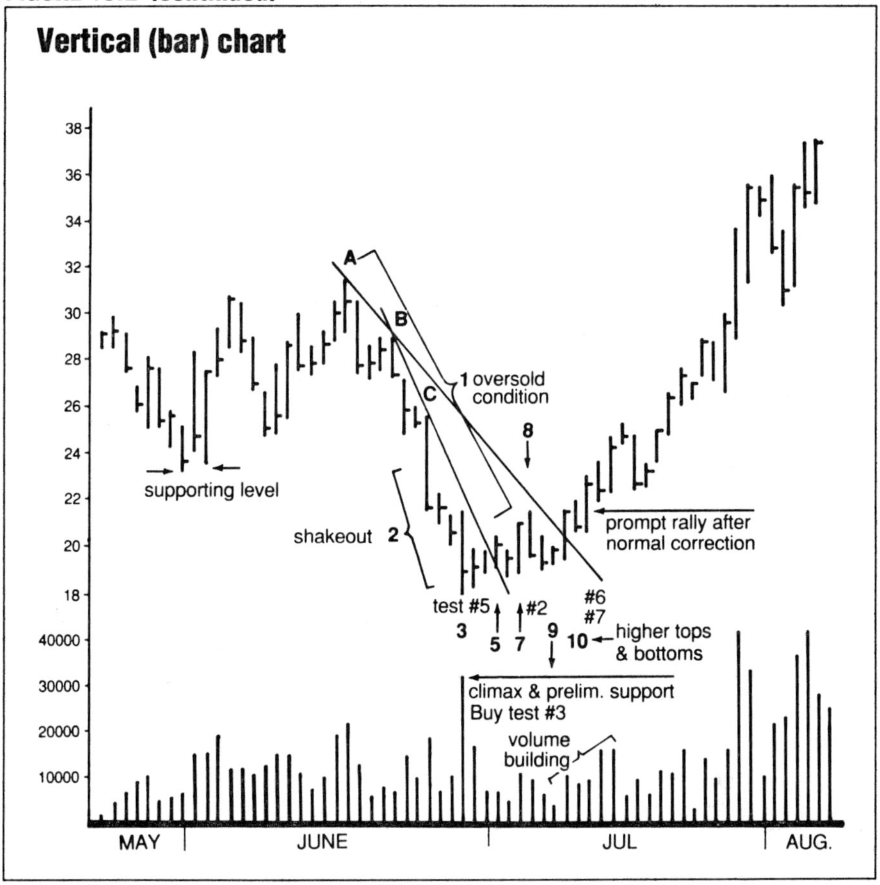

Buying and selling tests are applied to the one-point figure chart and the vertical bar chart of a hypothetical stock.

of you, test yourself by covering the right side of an unfamiliar chart and revealing the action day by day as if you were watching it unfold in real time. With practice, as we have said from the start, the principles of Wyckoff analysis will soon become second nature.

11
Maximizing Profits with Stop Orders

No matter what technical system you use, the first rule of successful trading and investing is: Cut your losses short. No one believed more firmly in this sage advice than Richard Wyckoff.

"No one can trade or invest without losses," he said. "Danger is present in every trade, whether it be for investment or speculation. In the stock market you must be constantly on your guard: Always expect something to happen."

Stop orders, in Wyckoff's view, are the mark of a professional attitude that acknowledges the ability to falter and the wisdom of money management. Stop orders also are an aid to judgment, allowing the trader and the investor to operate with less concern and more mental poise.

As an essential part of his method, Wyckoff insisted that traders and investors make a commitment only if the probable profit exceeds the potential risk by 3 to 1, that stop orders be used on every single transaction, whether long or short, and that the stop order price be determined before a commitment is made.

STOP ORDER BASICS

Stop orders are insurance that little losses will not run into big ones, that your working capital won't be tied up in losers.

There's nothing mysterious about a stop order. It's simply an instruction to a broker to sell long or buy short 100 shares of a stock when the price reaches a price you stipulate.

If you buy stock long at $50 per share and want to limit the loss to two points, the stop order is to sell 100 shares at 47-7/8 stop. If the price touches 47-7/8, the broker sells the shares at the market price as close as possible to 47-7/8.

Likewise, if you're buying short at 50 and want to limit the risk to 2 points, the order is to buy 100 at 52-1/8 stop. If the price rises to 52-1/8, the broker covers, or buys back, the shares at the best price after the stock hits 52-1/8. Whether you are trading odd lots (less than 100 shares) or round lots (100 shares), the stop will be executed based on round lot price.

Stop orders also are generally considered good till canceled, or GTC. You may prefer to specify that your stop orders are good this week (GTW) or good this month (GTM). This way, you needn't remember to cancel a GTC order after you've changed your positions, but you must remember to renew a GTW or GTM order on time.

Like any other aspect of dealing in the stock market, a sophisticated use of stop orders requires study. Moving stop orders while a trade is in motion can further reduce risk and maximize profit. The price at which stop orders are placed can influence the frequency with which they're caught. Determining the exact stop order price involves trained chart analysis.

Wyckoff advises that stop orders be placed at fractional prices because there usually is an accumulation of orders at even figures such as 90, 83, or 55. Market manipulators will try to get a stock up or down to even figures if it is to their advantage to see stop orders fulfilled and the traders taken out of the market.

Next to full figures, the half points are most often stated in stop orders. Quarter points are next in popularity and least of all the 3/8, 5/8 fractions. Therefore, it can be advantageous to place stops on long trades at the odd fractions below the even figure, and on short trades at the odd fraction above the even figure.

Stops, in Wyckoff's view, are not arbitrarily placed two or three points from every transaction price. Instead, the stop order should correspond to a logical "danger point." That danger point may be one to five points under a support level or one to five points above a resistance level, as determined by chart analysis. It may be the same number of points above or below a 50% reaction or rally mark. It can be the same number of points under a clearly defined support or supply line. The choice depends on the situation.

As a rule of thumb, the transaction price determines the number of points the stop price is placed from the danger point. Stops on very high-priced stocks would be in the 3- to 5-point range, 2-3 points on moderately priced stocks, and 1-2 points on low-priced stocks selling under $50.

The type of trading also governs the number of points at risk with a stop order. In short swing trading, where the goal is to profit from 3- to 5-point moves, the initial stop must be placed closer to the danger point and moved more quickly to reduce risk than if the goal is to catch intermediate price swings of 10 to 20 points, where you don't want to be kicked out of your position on minor reversals of a larger trend.

MOVING STOP ORDERS

Another rule of thumb is to move a stop 1/2 to 3/4 of a point from the transaction price as soon it can be done without additional risk in order to cover brokerage commissions. The stop would be moved above the transaction price on a long trade and below the transaction price on a short sale.

After a stock has moved well away from the point at which you took your initial position, whether long or short, you must remember that it is coming closer to a reaction or a rally or a turning point for a swing in the opposite direction. The more the stock moves in your favor, the closer your stop order should be moved to the market price.

Wyckoff advocates crowding the stop order right behind the

FIGURE 11.1

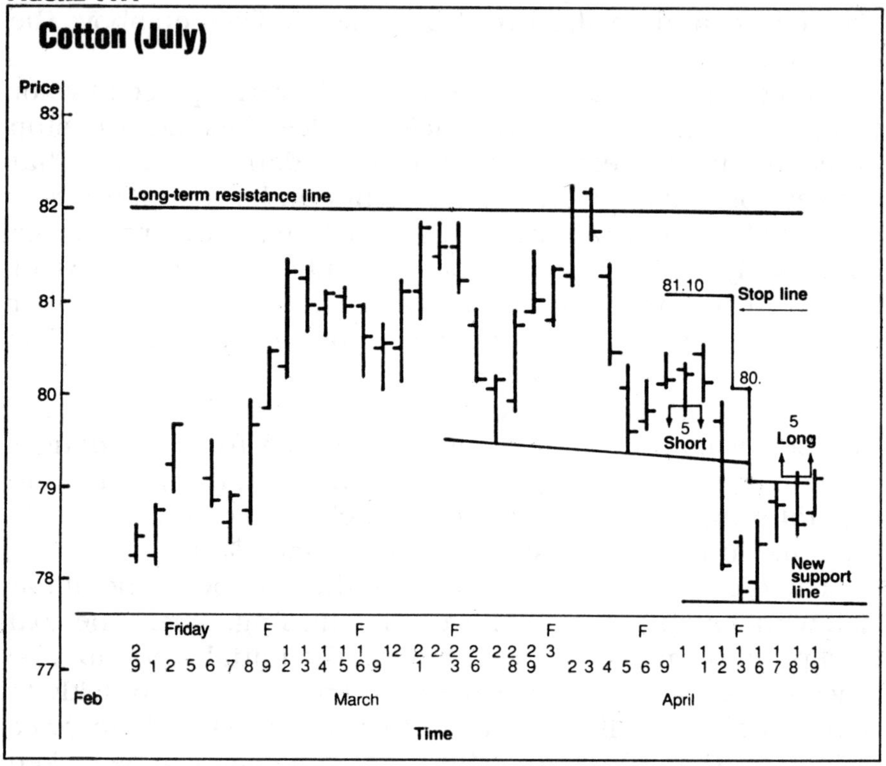

By using stops, this short trade made money. Cotton proceeded higher to reach 86.25 for a $7,000-per-contract move. Stops are not to be placed in an arbitrary fashion. Stops should be placed at a logical "danger point."

market price if the stock is 3-5 points from the completion of its indicated move. "Don't hold out for the last point," he would admonish his followers. He advises that the more a stock hesitates and seems ready to reverse, the closer the stop should be to the current market price.

In these instances, a stop moved to within one point of market price assures most of the paper profit already accrued, yet the way is still open for more profit. If stops were not employed and the trade simply closed out for fear of a reversal, the possibility of further profits would be closed.

Stops, however, are not short-cut substitutes for good

judgment. Good judgment closes out long trades on an upwave and short trades on the downswing. Stops take you out in a weaker position. From a practical point of view, however, the profit differential between closing out yourself and being closed out by a stop is not so much a loss as it is an operating expense — the cost of experience or the insurance premium to guard against larger losses.

A variation of the stop order is the "office stop" and "buy stop." Basically, you are asking the broker to begin your long or short transaction when the market price reaches a certain level. This is advisable only for those with a great deal of experience, who know exactly what they intend to accomplish and fully comprehend the dangers. This type of order is most useful when an important move without a material reversal is in the offing and must be caught as soon as it appears. Usually this is when a stock is ready to step on the springboard or is on a hinge.

The disadvantage is that the risk begins as soon as the trade is made for you and you must place immediately a conventional stop order to protect the purchase. This normally means a wider unprotected range between transaction price and secondary stop order — greater risk should the market misbehave.

FREQUENTLY CAUGHT STOPS

Wyckoff is adamant that stop orders be used with every transaction, whether for trade or investment. Investors, especially, he admonishes against carrying stock through losing periods, since a 10-point profit ensured by a stop order is more than could be taken out of most stocks by holding them for a full year's dividends.

If stops are caught too frequently, there are three probable reasons: 1) starting trades too soon (either through impatience to wait for reasonably conclusive indications or failure to decide in advance where the danger point exists and whether the profit potential outweighs the risk), 2) bucking the market trend, or 3) improperly placing and moving the stops.

If this happens to you, review your judgments about

potential market movements and about danger points. In any case, do not abandon the use of stops. If your stops continue to be caught too frequently, close out all your commitments, get out of the market, and stay out until you've located the source of your difficulty.

Rather than becoming irritated at such a situation, be thankful. The stop orders are sending a clear message that something in your technique is out of kilter. Persisting to defy the market would only damage your bank account, your confidence, and your ultimate success.

12
Intraday Swings with Wave Charts

The serious follower of Wyckoff, a trader who embraces the entire scope and intricate details of this methodology, has not completed his or her analytic arsenal without the Wyckoff Wave, a price vs. time chart that tracks intraday swings much like a doctor taking a patient's pulse.

Whether you trade by the hour or the year, it's the intraday swings, where bears and bulls test each other's strengths and weaknesses minute by minute, that grow and merge into the minor, intermediate-, and longest-term trends of most profit taking. By revealing this innermost working of the market, the wave chart frequently warns its reader of upcoming trend changes several days to a week before they would become apparent in the composite averages. It provides vital information for determining technical position and timing commitments. On a more intuitive level, its use heightens the trader's innate sense of critical market changes and important turning points.

In mastering the wave chart, traders seek to substantially

increase the accuracy of their judgment and transaction timing by better understanding how the market signals trend changes before they are well under way.

For traders without the time or inclination to study the market as it actually unfolds each trading day, the wave chart is a condensed, easily understood record of significant changes in supply and demand that can be studied at leisure. The chart also can be prepared at leisure, since its purpose is not to make intraday trading decisions, but to forewarn traders of impending interday moves. A number of sources provide intraday price data in various forms: *The Wall Street Journal*, on-line data transmission services, brokerages, the Chicago Mercantile Exchange yearbook, and the Stock Market Institute in Phoenix that teaches the Wyckoff method are just a few.

Graphically, a wave chart is a zigzag line representing the cumulative price that five leading stocks reach each time intraday buying and selling waves hit their peaks and valleys. Leading stocks are used, since the market seldom moves contrary to the trend of the leaders for a great while, and seldom more than temporarily. In most cases, important market movements start with these stocks — and practically no important move starts without these stocks being affected immediately. The five stocks are selected based on their activity and influence in the most recent months, and the roster is adjusted as often as necessary to keep the chart at the forefront of market trends.

In constructing a wave chart (Figure 12.1), the cumulative price of the leading stocks, measured in fractions, runs up the vertical scale. Time, measured in minutes, runs along the horizontal axis and marks the duration of each intraday swing. A fully illustrated wave chart also displays what Wyckoff calls "activity," or the rate at which orders flow into the market. Activity is an index measuring the size of lot orders — whether the market is moving due to the 100-share lots of public trading or the 1,000-share lots of professional market manipulation. Volume, although not illustrated on the chart, is a vital part of wave chart interpretation and is usually contained in a data table alongside the chart.

Building a wave chart starts with the total price of the five leading stocks at market opening. As soon as the first wave — either up or down — exhausts itself, the trader marks the time to the nearest five minutes and calculates the total highest or lowest price the indicator stocks reached at that time, including fractions.

If a stock price does not respond to the prevailing trend, if its price declines on an upwave or advances during a downwave, it's regarded as a delayed transaction rather than a contrary movement. The summation, at that point, uses the price the contrary stock reached on the previous wave. When the stock's price comes into line with the prevailing trend, the total is adjusted to reflect the price in accordance with the true trend.

This process continues until the market closes and the day's wave chart is completed by marking the five stocks' total closing price for the day, which then becomes the starting point for the next day's charting.

As part of his advisory service, Wyckoff provided his subscribers with wave charts and commentary on their movements. He valued the wave chart because, as he told his students, "Learn to judge small daily movements, and then you will be able to apply the same reasoning to the 3- to 5-point swings; to the 10-, 20-, and 30-point swings; and finally to the great swings that run over a period of years. In time, you will become proficient in all kinds of markets."

You can think of a wave chart as an exploded view of each bar on the vertical chart, much the same as a state road map enlarges the view of a major city's thoroughfares. In reading intraday waves, Wyckoff suggests that students first learn to interpret price movement and wave duration. Slight increases in distance and time warn the Wyckoff trader to be on the lookout for change.

As a simple example, let's assume the market has just opened and first sustains a 20-minute upwave that lifts the five leading stock prices a total of three points. This is followed by a 15-minute downwave that loses two points. The downwave's effect on price is less than the upwave's and its duration is shorter. Buying power contained in the upwave is obviously

FIGURE 12.1 Intraday bar chart and swing charts

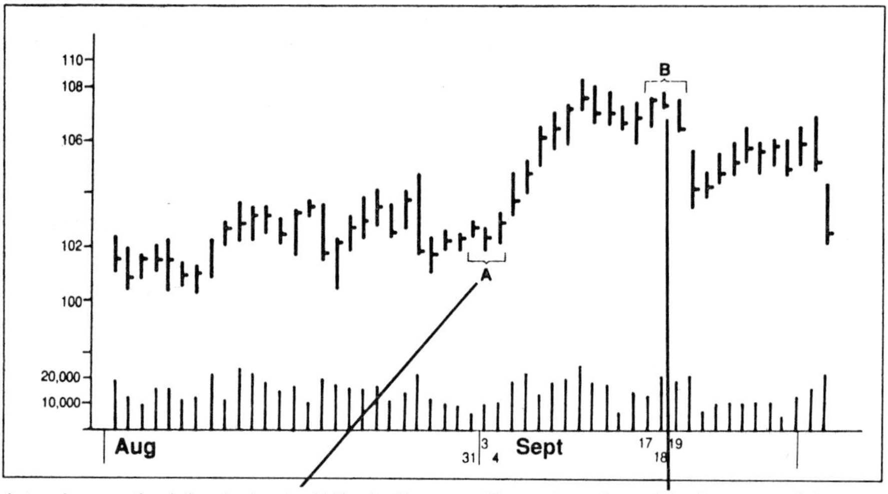

Intraday vertical (bar) chart of Wyckoff wave. The price plotted is the sum of the top five issues within an industry group.

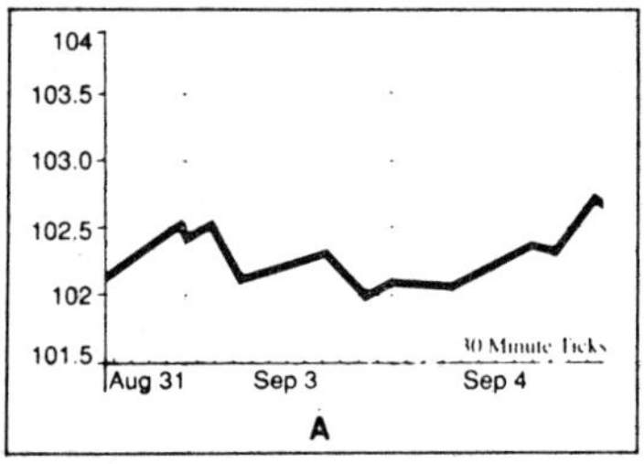

Intraday swing chart of Wyckoff wave bottom.

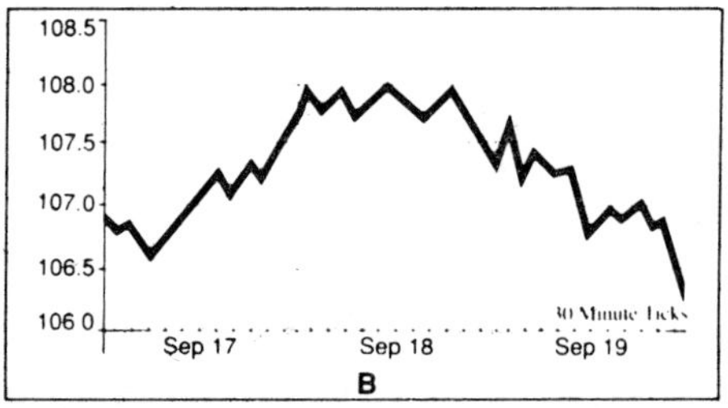

Intraday swing chart of Wyckoff wave top.

Intraday wave charts can assist the trader in recognizing a shift in strength to the demand side (A) or to the supply side (B) of a market.

stronger than the selling pressure contained in the downwave. Demand is greater than supply.

Suppose the next upswing lasts 45 minutes and carries the total stock price four points higher than its previous upwave. This signals an apparent increase in buying power. The ensuing reaction, which lasts 20 minutes and drops prices 1-

1/2 points, confirms the buying power, since this second downwave lasted five minutes longer than the first downwave and produced less price change.

The additional information of intraday volume and Wyckoff's intraday measure of activity gives the trader a better handle on upcoming price movements. The volume, or amount of stock, that market participants are willing to trade at a certain price is a strong indication of the bullishness or bearishness of the immediate future. Volume that follows the price trend is usually bullish; volume that runs counter to the price trend is usually bearish. In other words, increased volume with rising prices or decreased volume with declining prices is bullish. Increased volume with declining prices or decreased volume with rising prices is bearish. In either case, a sudden and abnormally large volume can indicate the approach or culmination of a move.

Activity fine-tunes this judgment by telling a trader more about the "quality" of the volume — whether it's made up of many public traders buying or selling small lots of 100 shares or less, or whether volume is the result of large traders moving 1,000-share and larger lots. Heavy public trading is considered poor quality volume, since the public doesn't have the financial clout to manipulate the market and can only follow what large-scale traders set up. It helps the Wyckoff analyst understand whether manipulators are in the midst of a campaign or winding one up. For example, it's important to know whether low volume means offerings are scarce because they were bullishly sopped up in large lots in a preceding reaction or if it signifies the poor quality of small public lots and further decline. Likewise, is rallying volume the result of short covering or an engineered attempt to unload stocks before a major decline gets underway?

However, when analyzing intraday moves, don't expect every daily chart to send a clear, unconfused message. The market's actions for several days may be indecisive. What is vital about the wave chart is the cumulative impression it builds about the longer trends, the wider price swings. At important turning points, the intraday swings will convey vital information about the market's critical condition.

Wyckoff recommends that casual observation, not mathematical comparison, is the way to approach a wave chart and that the analyst not waste effort or create confusion by making volume and activity comparisons when the market is not displaying critical behavior.

The relationships of price, duration, volume, and activity are especially important when price approaches former levels of support and resistance. Figure charts created from the wave chart — Wyckoff recommends a 1-point, a 3- to 5-point chart for intermediate swings and a 10-point chart for the largest trends — will help indicate whether large-scale operators are nearing their price objectives.

As a rule of thumb, successive failures to rally beyond former highs or to drop through former lows warns of impending, important trend changes. It is accumulating evidence of a change from strength to weakness or vice versa. Together, the wave and figure charts will illustrate the situation in graphic detail.

It's clear, therefore, that trading long trends shouldn't limit technical analysis to the same time frame. Digging into the smallest of the market's actions and reactions can teach a trader important lessons about lifting power vs. selling pressure, the market's responsiveness or lack of it to rotation of supply and demand, the speed of advances and declines, and what changes in activity and volume reveal about the character of buying and selling.

13
Serving an Apprenticeship

It is the clear intent of any student of the stock market to move themselves away from those who rely on luck as their *modus operandi.* A true student of the market doesn't graduate into actual trading before he or she completes a self-imposed apprenticeship wherein experience becomes the teacher.

Experience hones practical skills such as the timing of trades and also helps develop the mental attitude that allows a trader or investor to think clearly and follow an analysis to its conclusion. If you, as a student of the Wyckoff method, were embarking into an apprenticeship alone, experience could be a hard and painful lesson. But Wyckoff offers a comprehensive package of detours around the common pitfalls that so often lead novice technical analysts into frustration.

Here we'll discuss how to approach practical skills, and later examine the mental and emotional attributes a technical analyst should encourage.

Paper Trading

Medical students don't begin their apprenticeships with heart transplants, and stock market students don't jump right into trading with their hard-earned capital. Trading on paper is the inexpensive way to gain experience and test abilities.

Although paper profits aren't as thrilling as cold cash profits, early success on paper should bring a thrill in achievement and in knowing that you never again have to take chances or suffer disastrous losses.

Paper trading should continue until you learn what and when to buy or sell—anywhere from 50 to 100 transactions. Use stop orders and keep records just as if you were working with a broker. Figure commissions and taxes; calculate net profit and loss.

Be certain of your judgment before you venture a dollar in the market, and don't let anyone entice you into hastily committing real money. In the beginning, knowledge of stock market technique is far more valuable than capital.

Actual Trading

When you feel confident enough to trade with money, start with 10- or 15-share lots, no matter how large your capital. You're still in training, so don't try to make money at this stage by overtrading and piling extra nervous strain on your judgment.

Operating with actual money is more of a test of your ability than paper trading, because, says Wyckoff, "when your money is at stake you will be more or less at the mercy of the two devils of stock market followers—hope and fear."

Diversify into three, five, 10 or 20 of your best selections, depending on your capital and ability to watch each commitment. Resist the temptation to put all your faith in 100 shares of one stock vs. 20 shares of five issues. Out of five issues, one may fail, one may not turn out as well as expected, but the other three should more than compensate for the others. "The man does not live who can make a profit on every transaction."

All commitments need not be made at once, of course, but Wyckoff does advise that trades be made in the same number of shares (equal lots) of each stock. Loading up on low-priced stocks, the most speculative and riskiest, would mean losing trades most often occurring in the largest lots, while profits come in small amounts from higher-priced stocks.

If you're investing for intermediate and major swings, you also could divide your capital by investing the same number of dollars in each issue — provided you stick to the higher-grade stocks and do not put an undue percentage of funds into low-priced stocks.

Any profits made at the start should be used to build up your capital for dealing later in larger lots. If you spread your capital too thin in the beginning, you may be handicapped and discouraged by early experience. If actual results aren't as good as your paper-trading results, go back to paper.

WORK AND STUDY HABITS

Find a quiet spot away from interruptions to study your paper and actual transactions. Whether it's your home den, your office after hours, or a privately leased office, find someplace far from brokers, gossip, questions, and rumors that will confuse judgment.

Devote at least one hour each day to studying the market. You can obtain the comparatively few facts needed to compile your own records from an evening newspaper's stock pages. As Wyckoff explains: "The best results I ever had in judging the market and trading were when I could devote only one hour a day to study of the market, planning my campaigns and giving instructions, and so busily engaged in other affairs that it prevented my studying the [ticker] tape throughout the session."

In Wyckoff's view, it is much better to make one commitment a month that realizes a profit than to trade every day and show a net loss.

Concentrate on determining the position of the market, defining its trend, anticipating turning points, and selecting stocks that should make the most profit in the shortest time. The study should become almost like comparing successive snapshots of a moving object, much like time-lapse photography.

LEARN TO SELL SHORT

Selling short is not as easy for most people as trading on the long side. But the biggest and quickest money is on the short side.

Trade on paper until you can sell short as easily as go long. "A trader who can only operate on one side of the market is only half a trader," says Wyckoff. "He sees everything through the eyes of a bull. He thinks everything is always going up. He never can see money on the short side. The truth is, a chronic bear has a better chance of making money than a chronic bull."

TIME YOUR ACTIONS CAREFULLY

Don't jump in too soon and tie up money waiting for a stock to move up or down. Wait for the period of preparation to end, and let other people play with the stock until then.

Go with stock that should move soonest, farthest, and fastest. You want immediate action for your money, and it is bad practice to hold a position for many days or weeks without getting anything out of it.

LIMIT LOSSES AND LET PROFITS RUN

This is a fundamental Wall Street principle that the public notoriously practices in reverse because the public forgets that it's not what you make, but what you keep, that counts.

Decide in advance how much risk is in a trade. Profits should be at least several times the amount of risk before it's considered worthwhile and a stop order should always be used to limit losses. It's no sin to be wrong, but disastrous to let a small loss run into big figures.

Know every minute why you are starting a trade, why you're holding it, and why you should close out. If your stops are caught too frequently, use more discrimination in starting trades. Refuse all but the best opportunities and wait for them.

PLACING ORDERS

In nearly every case, whether long or short, it's best to place your orders "at the market." If you specify a price, a broker may not be able to get the stock at that exact price and you may miss an entire move.

Limited orders (the office stop and buy stop, where a new trade is to begin at a specific price) can be useful if you are experienced enough to anticipate an action. One example is if you clearly anticipate a slight dip in price that would be an advantageous buying position before a stock continues advancing. Don't "straddle" the market (being long in one stock and short in another) unless you are so proficient and so controlled that nothing will rattle you.

Work in harmony with the indicated market trends and wait for the best openings; don't try to jump into every turn. If the market indicates a decline, go short. When the decline runs its course, cover and watch for signs of an important reversal. Then go long, and when that important rally has topped out, read the market for signs of a continuing decline to switch back to short selling.

Wyckoff also advises against timing a long or short trade according to the ex-dividend date (the date dividends are declared) simply to obtain the dividend payment. The allure of this practice in a bull market is that the amount of the dividend frequently will be recovered in the stock's price within a day or two following the ex-dividend date. Likewise, in a bear market, the stock price may sag off by the amount of the dividend and lose several more points due to offerings from those who held the stock just for dividends. Yet, in both cases, this is gambling for a gain that is absorbed in the long run by the average trend.

Pyramiding

This technique of adding shares of stock to a position for each point the stock moves in your favor is comparatively safe only under certain conditions. The ideal time for pyramiding on the short side is when pressure is so heavy and support so light that it signals a sudden and drastic decline. On the long side, it is when sudden and insistent demand creates such an irresistible lifting power that the stock seems about to be driven suddenly and strongly upward.

Wyckoff advises that pyramiding isn't justified without the

potential for a 10- to 15-point move, and that orders to buy or sell additional lots should be limit orders so the broker executes the commitments automatically.

One way to pyramid is to make the initial commitment, say, of 300 shares, with a stop order 3 points or less from the price. For each point the market in your favor, add a certain number of shares, in this case 100, with a 3-point-or-less stop order. Move the stop on the initial commitment (lower if short, higher if long) for each point the stock moves favorably. Move the stops on the smaller, subsequent lots so that none of them surpasses the initial stop.

Averaging

Never increase your line if a trade goes against you. Letting a stock run against you more than a few points is bad practice, but "letting it run" to where it seems more desirable to buy or sell more in order to average the cost is worse.

A losing stock proves wrong judgment, and a stop order should get you out with a small loss. Why abandon the stop and persist in using wrong judgment?

Closing trades

There should be as good a reason for closing a trade as there is for beginning it in the first place, and both should be based on your chart or ticker tape analysis. If you begin a trade based on chart indications, finish the trade based on the chart. Likewise, a trade begun with a tape indication should be closed based on the tape.

If analysis indicates "neutrality," close your commitment whether there is a profit or loss in it and stand aside until there are definite indications of a move up or down.

How well you're able to follow Wyckoff's practical advice is greatly influenced by the mental attitude you cultivate. Complete self-control, unhindered by emotion, is the stock trader's perfect mental state; how to approach that type of intellectual calm is the subject of our next chapter.

14
Developing a Personal Trading Style

"A stock market operator must be as hard-boiled as a five-minute egg; cold-blooded as a fish; deaf to all gossip; blind to news; and dumb as a door knob when it comes to discussing the market with others." — Richard D. Wyckoff

Trading the stock market with the Wyckoff method is as much a test of personality and personal perseverance as it is a test of analytic education. Wyckoff was strictly a loner when it came to studying and trading the stock market. He believed the best way, the only way, his students would become profitable technical analysts was to rely on their own intelligence and to develop an inner fortitude against inevitable mistakes.

To his way of thinking, mastering the technical aspects of his method was only half the battle of working the stock market. Controlling emotional fervor and keeping a clear head when actually applying the technical know-how in a not-so-perfect market was the other half. Traders or investors wouldn't be able to do that, he felt, if they were continually looking for advice from others or if their technical reasoning was poisoned with rumors and news reports.

Brokerage houses in particular were his bane. He warned against eavesdropping on the gossip, making quick looks at the ticker, or listening to unsolicited recommendations from brokers. "Be self reliant," he advised. "Never ask your broker or anyone else what they think of the market. Make it a rule that your broker only quotes prices when you specifically ask for them. Make it a rule that the broker does nothing more than take the order and confirm its execution. Form your own opinion and try to make it so accurate that you gain confidence in yourself."

Wyckoff was quite intent on his students developing their own judgment, self-reliance, courage, prudence, pliability, and patience. "We can train you to develop good judgment," he said, "but you must train yourself to act upon your decisions and to carry them to a successful conclusion." Success, he said, requires that "you operate with no emotions whatever. Be as indifferent, hard-boiled and levelheaded in opening and closing actual commitments as you would if they were merely paper trades. You'll be surprised to find how greatly (complete emotional control) strengthens your judgment."

As a start, he recommended that each student "make a searching analysis of your own mental processes. Study your psychological shortcomings. To know them is to beat them." Above all, he admonished against wasting time regretting losses or lost opportunities. "The only value of a mistake is the lesson it may teach; the only thought you will give to your errors will be studying the reasons for them."

Wyckoff was a firm believer in "playing a lone hand" and drawing conclusions without the consultation of "experts," because every person views the market from a slightly different vantage point. One expert may interpret price and volume movements from an investor's standpoint and another from a day-to-day trading outlook. The trader who is dependent on another person's opinions will not only fail to understand the market, he felt, but could very well be thrown off a proper course by offhand and conflicting opinions.

Realistically, though, Wyckoff did acknowledge the existence and lure of advisory services even in the 1930s. It went against his grain, but he said, "If you must use an advisory service, check up on their recommendations...and don't hesitate to disagree."

He was a prudent market player, too. He believed that staying out of the market was as much a strategic move as being in it. "Never get the idea you must be in the market all the time," he counseled. "In fact, plan to be completely liquid at intervals to prevent yourself from going stale, and to keep a fresh, clear perspective."

He explained several clear signals warning to pull out of the market. The first is a technical warning—the situation in which the trader's analysis gives unclear, confused signals. The other two are emotional warnings—relying on "instinct" rather than research and a growing or chronic indecisiveness about executing trades.

His advice was to never go into a stock because you think it may do well and never make a commitment until you've thoroughly studied its position, background, and present behavior.

If at any time you find yourself powerless to move because you haven't the nerve to trade, he advised making trades on paper until confidence returned. Better still, he said, "take a vacation from the market. Do nothing for some days or weeks. When you return to it, you will find your judgment improved."

He especially advocated stringent measures "whenever you find hope or fear warping judgment. Close out all positions at the market price regardless of profit or loss. Stay out of the market for a few days, a week or longer until these two emotions that cause so many failures subside."

Wyckoff's experience led him to the conclusion that being in the market at all times is not the key to profits. Being in the market when there is a clear, unconfused technical signal and the trader's judgment is not swayed by emotion was his rule for success.

The first emotional juggernaut traders or investors must

deal with is the matter of risking capital. Working the stock market requires the courage to lose money, but risking more than you can afford to lose will warp judgment. Equally destructive and ill-fated, as Wyckoff points out, is an obsession with amassing a fortune overnight.

For both these reasons, Wyckoff counseled his students to first venture a fraction of their capital—say $1,000 out of a total $10,000 trading fund—in a series of trades in small amounts of stock. Learn to play the game professionally instead of trying to make an instant killing, he told them. Don't allow actual or potential success in the early stages lure you into trading too large a proportion of capital. And, he reiterated, until you can be calm and collected with the amount of capital at risk, continue to practice on paper and hone your skills for the real campaign

Flexibility is another essential skill Wyckoff felt that anyone in the stock market should develop. "Don't get fixed on a certain amount of profit you hope to make on any commitment. The charts will indicate the possibilities...but the market situation can change in 24 hours."

Once you've made up your mind the market is topping out, he added, don't be in a hurry to climb back into a stock out of which you have just taken a substantial profit. "Let the other guy gamble for the last eighth of a point," he advised.

In Wyckoff's mind, too, patience equals greater profits. This is the patience to wait for opportunities to develop and to wait for clear signals from the charts. "Don't be in a hurry to get into the market simply because you have surplus cash" was his advice. "Wait until you see a real opportunity. One good commitment a year will make profits of many times the interest you could earn on your money for a few months outside the market...but one hasty trade can set you back an entire year's interest plus the shock to your confidence."

Wyckoff believed in committing capital to the market when stocks were ready to make their swiftest and furthest moves. The patience to wait for these situations, however, didn't demand 100% certainty before taking action. "By that time," he said, "your move will have started and the opportunity slipped away. Don't run after the move that has escaped—your judgment will be biased by your first error and chances are you won't act with a clear mind. Look around for the next opportunity."

He also cautioned against mixing technical methods. If a trade is made based on ticker tape indications, close the trade on that basis. If a chart is the basis for taking a position, the chart should be the reason for finishing out the position. Don't confuse the techniques of short-swing trading with intermediate-trend trading. And don't, he warned, drop by the broker's office at lunch to see how the market's behaving. It will be just one paragraph, not the whole story that your analysis will show.

Wyckoff, likewise, believed in one trading method—his method. He saw no reason to clutter it up with other ideas and theories (especially the Dow Theory). "Our instruction is practical, founded on principles employed by real operators and not beautiful theories. It is complete in itself; it covers all requirements in all phases of the market. It has been tested in all kinds of markets for more than 25 years, and the underlying principles are as old as the market itself."

15 Market Strategy

The reasoning behind Richard Wyckoff's classic method of chart analysis is simple and straightforward: when demand for a stock exceeds supply, prices rise; when supply is greater than demand, prices decline. The goal of this method is to make the most efficient use of investment capital by selecting only issues that will move soonest, fastest and farthest in any market and by timing trades to capture those moves.

The Wyckoff method accomplishes this by working in harmony with the market's buying and selling waves, not against them. The search is for turning points that an individual feels comfortable trading — anything from the final top of a bull market to the intraday peaks and valleys of buying and selling waves.

The system evolved during Wyckoff's years in the stock market, a time when experience was the only stock market teacher. As a broker, Wyckoff watched traders with financial clout make their behind-the-scenes plays and realized the market's future could be discerned from the price and volume that gave away the plans of those who dominated trading. He published his method, the first technical analysis of its kind, in 1908 and began publishing weekly forecasts based on his analysis in 1911.

Although the Wyckoff method relies solely on price and volume charts, it is far from a purely mechanical or mathematical system. Wyckoff intended that his students use charts to gain a feel for the push and pull of supply and demand. He saw an analyst as someone who uncovered the human forces behind price and volume fluctuations, not a rote technician drawing lines and angles.

Manipulator campaigns

In Wyckoff's view, charts reveal the activity that is the product of market manipulation by knowledgeable and influential traders. A Wyckoff analyst, therefore, can look at any chart and visualize an "aggregate manipulator" who undertakes a four-phase campaign of market manipulation.

The first phase is "accumulation," in which a large operator acquires a line of stock at the lowest possible prices. Here, supply grows scarce and demand builds to give prices the power to rise later. Accumulation is a lengthy process. It comes across on vertical charts as sideward price movement, a "congestion area," that shows no tendency to take off in either direction and is accompanied by consistently low volume. This phase also may contain some drastic downturns to shake stock out of the hands of tenacious holders and into the operator's portfolio.

The next phase, "marking up," occurs when the operator has all the targeted stock in hand. The operator allows the price to rise or gives it a push with well-placed bids either gradually or swiftly. On the vertical chart, marking up is a series of fast price upthrusts alternating with momentary plateaus or "resting spells," accompanied by rising volume.

The third phase is "distribution," where the operator buys and sells from the accumulated line to give it the appearance of strength and catch public attention. On the charts, this comes across as a "congestion area," a range where price seems to have settled. The stable trading range is intended to fool the public into thinking the stock is waiting to take off again. In reality, the operator is unloading the stock, taking profits and ready to start "marking down," the last phase in which price is allowed to fall naturally. Here, the operator takes a short position in preparation for a major decline.

CHARTS

The Wyckoff method uses three types of charts — vertical line (bar), figure (point & figure) and a wave chart Wyckoff developed to forewarn of turning points. At the very minimum, an experienced Wyckoff trader can chart the stock market with a daily financial newspaper, a notebook and an hour a day in a quiet place.

To avoid spending too much time charting and not enough analyzing, the Wyckoff analyst maintains vertical charts of the composite and important group averages and figure charts of individual stocks. At the same time, the analyst scans individual stock volumes in a daily financial journal, looking for surges that would give cause for further investigation.

The search is for groups that are weak when the market is strong (buyers have reason to believe they can sell higher later on) and groups that are strong when the market is weak (buyers know something to the group's disadvantage and are selling out).

From vertical charts, which follow price and volume, the analyst learns which direction prices are moving, whether it's an opportune time for buying, selling or closing out and where to place stop orders. Figure charts show only price changes and are used to forecast the approximate number of points a stock should move. They also help the analyst see where supply or support is building and how far a correction or rally moves.

When vertical group charts show promise that a group could move further and faster than the composite, the analyst refers to the figure charts of individual stocks to evaluate the size of potential price moves. This information comes from the figure chart's "horizontal formation" — a price that is repeated for a number of days and creates a horizontal baseline from which future prices advance or decline. The number of times

FIGURE 15.1

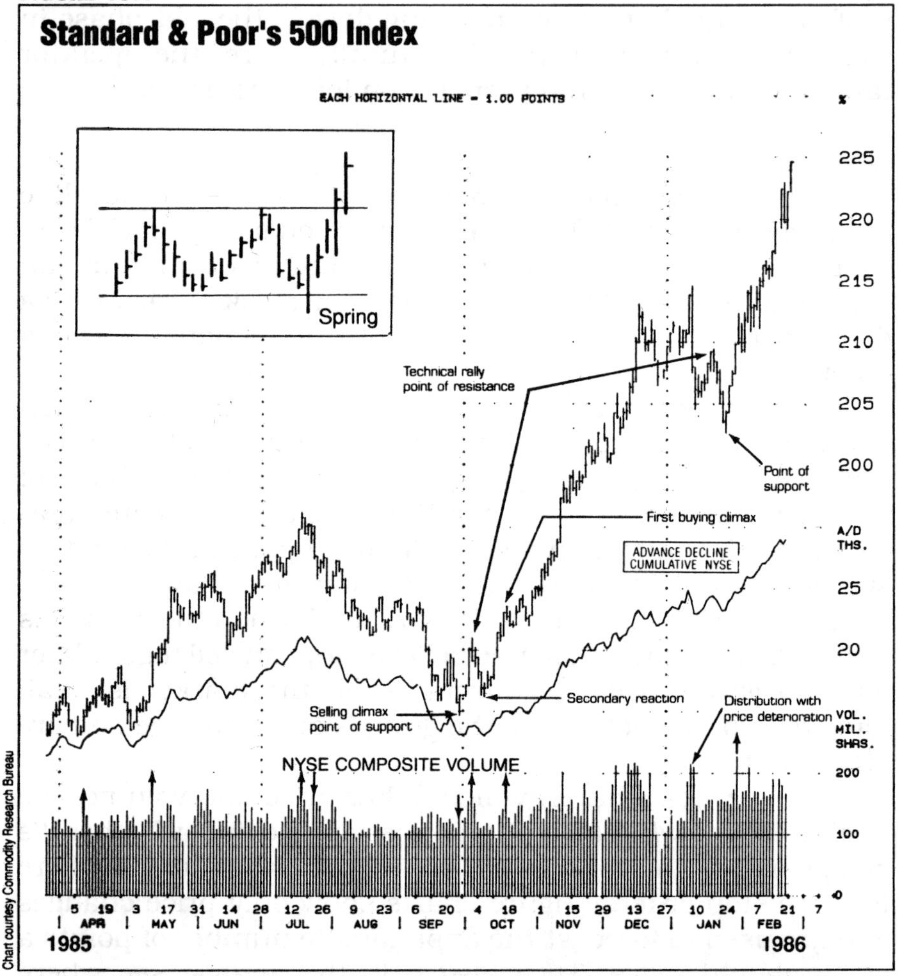

The Wyckoff method applies volume/price analysis to determine the overall health of the market. A market bottom is typically accompanied by a selling climax as weak hands liquidate their long positions to well-informed traders. Following a bottom is a technical rally due to a lack of supply. The secondary reaction (test of support) is accompanied by low volume. The lack of volume indicates that the available supply is in the hands of strong traders and a rally is forthcoming.

a price is repeated in the horizontal formation is the number of points a stock, a group, or the market should advance from its deepest low or decline from its peak high. A horizontal formation after a decline indicates that market manipulators are willing to support the stock and stem the decline. After a rally, a horizontal formation signals a downturn in prices as soon as supply satiates demand.

From the indications of group and composite vertical and individual figure charts, the analyst knows when it's time to construct vertical charts of promising individual stocks. For additional and extremely detailed information, the analyst can turn to Wyckoff's wave chart, which tracks the aggregate intraday price of five leading stocks vs. time. The wave chart is an exploded view of each bar on a vertical chart and is used to detect critical points in market action and, frequently, to warn of changes days before they are apparent on composite average charts.

BASIC CHART PATTERNS

Although the stock market rarely behaves exactly the same way twice, charts do follow general patterns that indicate imminent money-making opportunities. In a declining market, the usual chain of events is a selling climax, followed by a technical rally, then a secondary reaction. Rising markets follow a similar pattern, starting with a buying climax.

On a vertical chart, a sudden abnormally large volume as sellers unload their holdings gives the first signal that a selling climax is imminent. The price range usually drops and widens, the closing price hits nearer and nearer to the low. The selling actually climaxes on a day of high volume and a closing price near the high.

Immediately after the climax is the first chance to buy long. A stop order should be placed two or three points under the purchase price and one to two points under the climax low.

Customarily, a technical rally (automatic rally or rebound) follows in which volume dips and the price range jumps higher. If buyers during the climax did not intend to hold their purchases, those stocks will be thrown back on the market during the technical rally. Although the market looks bullish, it's the next phase, the secondary reaction (or test), that shows where the market is really headed.

When the rally's supply is too large for buyer demand, prices during the secondary reaction will drop lower than the extreme low of the selling climax and a new decline is in the offing. On the other hand, if the market reacts with shrinking volume and prices at or above the low of the selling climax, an upturn may be on the way.

Here is a second chance to buy long, after the secondary reaction shows that buyers are gaining the upper hand as volume retreats and prices hover above the climax low. In this situation, the market is on the "springboard," ready to advance.

The final confirmation of an important reversal is prices rising beyond the technical rally's extreme high. This is the third and least favorable chance to go long because a purchase would be amid an upwave rather than at a turning point. This increases risk, since the market may test the lows set during the selling climax and secondary reaction several times before a bull market really gets underway.

A CLOSER LOOK AT PRICE AND VOLUME

Today's market behavior means nothing until it's been compared with what happened in the past, and "support" and "resistance" points are essential clues to future performance. A support point is the lowest price set in the recent past; similarly, a resistance point is the highest price set in the recent past.

Usually, price will "hesitate" as it nears a support or resistance point. Breaching either of these points, especially when volume is increasing, is a significant event that demonstrates the strength of the trend. This makes support and resistance points useful levels for placing stop orders.

Another essential test of the market's technical strength or weakness is how far a price flops during a reaction or how far it rises during a rally. Normally, a reaction drops half the distance of the preceding rally and a rally rises half the distance of the preceding reaction. For example, a 10-point advance followed by a 54-point reaction is considered normal. A reaction of more than half indicates technical weakness — the trend may be fading. Conversely, a rise of more than half after a decline would be considered technical strength.

When a chart shows a pattern of rising prices that tend to flatten out or arch over, the chart indicates that demand is dying or supply is greater than buyers can handle. When a chart shows declining prices that level off or round upward, it's a message that supply is petering out.

The rate of price change gives important clues to impending action. Look for sudden sharp movements up or down (called thrusts and shakeouts) or a price that stops oscillating and comes to "dead center." A shakeout may look like an exaggerated selling climax on charts or a rapid drop at the end of an extensive preparation for advance. It is intended to scare stock out of the hands of persistent hangers-on. A thrust is the reverse of a shakeout, a sharp run up and out of an area of distribution or a temporary bulge through the top of a trading range to encourage buyers.

When price comes to dead center or a "hinge," however, it tells the analysts the stock is probably on the "springboard" and ready for sharp and immediate action where entry into the market makes most efficient use of capital. A springboard can also occur after preparations for distribution and becomes evident after price has declined and settled in a range.

Volume confirms or denies price clues. A gradual buildup of volume means the public is coming into an advancing market or leaving a declining one and gives price the momentum to continue its current direction.

Volume that follows the price trend is usually bullish (that is, increasing volume with rising prices or decreasing volume with declining prices). Volume that runs counter to the price trend is usually bearish.

Abnormally large and swift expansion of volume marks a turning point — either temporary or permanent. It heralds the approach or the culmination of a move.

Small or "light" volume is like the end of a chapter in a book:

Something new is in the offing. Light volume at the bottom of a decline of any size indicates that selling is drying up and taking the pressure off declining prices. Light volume at the top of a rise in price is usually bearish and indicates that demand has been filled and prices should drop.

TRENDLINES

Trendlines are drawn through the successive tops or bottoms of price on a vertical chart, so it is easier to see when prices are changing pace or reversing their direction. Any threatened violation of a trendline indicates that the force of demand or supply is weakening. An analyst, however, must use judgment in drawing trendlines and in interpreting how they are broken and the conditions under which violations occur.

There are four basic trendlines: a support line passing through two successive points of support in an uptrend; a supply line passing through two successive points or resistance in a downtrend; an oversold position line drawn parallel to the supply line and passing through the first point of support between the supply line's two tops; and an overpassing through the first point of resistance between the support line's two bottoms.

When price breaches a support or oversold line, it's a signal to buy long or cover shorts. Breaching a supply or overbought line indicates that it's time to sell out or go short.

By extending a trendline past the points that define it, the trader has a better idea of what can be expected of future prices.

POSITION SHEET

A position sheet is a record-keeping device that tracks the potential movements of individual stocks in each group. On the position sheet, each stock is in one of five positions — ready to make a short or long upward swing, a short or long downward swing, or no move at all.

The number of stocks in the bullish vs. the bearish positions gives the analyst an indication where the overall market sits and which groups are most closely aligned with the composite trend. From there, it's a matter of selecting individual stocks from the position sheets that are in harmony with the overall market and show the most price potential.

A summary of the position sheet is charted permanently as the technical positions barometer, which can then be used as a trend forecaster.

STOP ORDERS

Stop orders should be used on every transaction and their position determined before a commitment is made. It's advantageous to place stop orders at fractional prices because there usually is an accumulation of orders at full prices (i.e., 90 or 83) and at half points. On long trades, place stops at odd fractions below the full figure and, on short trades, at the odd fractions above the figure.

Stops should correspond to support and resistance levels. As a rule of thumb, stops would be in the 3- to 5-point range on high-priced stocks, 2-3 points on moderately price stocks, and 1-2 points on stocks selling under $50.

The shorter the trading cycle, too, the closer a stop should be placed to a support or resistance level and the faster it should be moved. The more a stock moves in your favor, the closer the stop order should be moved to the market price. By the time the market price is 3 to 5 points from a profit objective, the stop should be crowded right behind it.

When stops are caught too often, the trader is either starting trades too soon, bucking the market trend or placing and moving stops improperly.

SERVING AN APPRENTICESHIP

Trading requires both technical knowledge and emotional restraint, and Wyckoff helped his students master both.

On the technical side, he was a firm believer in serving an apprenticeship with paper trades before delving into the real market. It is the inexpensive way to gain experience and develop confidence. Wyckoff recommended at least 50 to 100 paper trades — on both the long and short sides — before venturing money in the market. That first venture should be a small, diversified portfolio of 10- or 15-share lots, no matter how much trading capital is available. Profits build up the capital for dealing in larger lots at a later time.

The best place to paper trade is in a quiet spot away from interruptions for at least an hour a day. Concentrate on determining the market's position and trend, anticipating turning points and selecting stocks that should move farthest and fastest.

Watch how you time transactions—don't jump in too soon; wait for the peak. Decide in advance how much risk is in a trade and know every minute why you are starting it, why you are holding it, and why you should close out.

Place your orders "at the market"; otherwise, you may miss an entire move because your broker can't get the stock exactly at a price you specify. Also, don't pyramid unless you have the potential for a 10- to 15-point move. Use limit orders when you buy or sell these additional lots, so the broker executes your orders automatically.

Never increase your line if a trade goes against you. Some traders will let a stock run to where it seems more desirable to buy or sell, trying to average the loss over more shares. A losing trade is the result of bad judgment, and why persist in using bad judgment?

On the emotional level, Wyckoff stressed self-reliance, self-confidence, and a "hard-boiled," analytical approach to managing trades. Particularly, he advised analysts to pull out of the market and regroup psychologically whenever they felt fear, hope, indecisiveness, or a tendency to rely on instinct entering into their decisions.

Troubleshooting Your Own Performance

At any point in your trading, it's a good idea to stop and analyze your past performance. Step back and take an objective view at losses or at trades that didn't quite work the way you thought they should. What went wrong? Does the same problem crop up again and again? Test yourself against this list of common errors:

- Making trades with insufficient study and practice
- Making trades out of harmony with the market trend
- Taking a position too late after a move is well under way or completed
- Taking a position too soon due to impatience
- Improperly estimating the distance a stock should move
- Letting eagerness to make profits warp judgment
- Failing to keep a position sheet and selecting stocks on hunches rather than calculations
- Buying on bulges instead of waiting for reactions
- Abandoning the use of vertical charts in favor of figure charts
- Buying after a stock has risen above the level where several buying indications appeared
- Failing to place and move stops
- Listening to advice from brokers, advisors, friends, or newsletters.

The answer to these problems is to return to paper trading for a while and to master the technical or emotional gremlins that are fouling up your trades. Don't be hasty in pronouncing yourself cured, either. As Wyckoff would have counseled, "Staying out of the market is as much a strategic move as being in it."

PART II

The Wyckoff Method in Action

by David H. Weis

1

The Wyckoff Method and Bond Futures

In 1908, Richard Wyckoff began publishing *The Ticker*, a monthly magazine designed to educate the public on how to understand and profit from the stock market. The early popularity of this magazine can be attributed to the series of articles that Wyckoff wrote on tape reading. He had spent 20 years on Wall Street and learned the secrets of the most successful traders who studied every transaction on the stock ticker. In describing James Keene, a successful syndicate manager, Wyckoff mentioned how he poured over the tape as if in a trance, analyzing "prices, volumes, and fluctuations down to the finest imaginable point."

Wyckoff, too, mastered the art of tape reading, which he defined as a "method for forecasting from what appears on the tape now, what is likely to appear in the future." By studying the flow of buy and sell orders into the marketplace, Wyckoff learned to recognize the behavior on the tape that revealed when large interests were building a position prior to a markup or markdown in price. This approach was discussed in Wyckoff's autobiography:

> Anyone who undertook to read (from the tape) the minds of the momentary buyers and sellers was able to measure, to a certain degree, their eagerness to sell or buy. Also, he was able to measure the force of the buying or selling power as shown by the number of shares (volume). He could also judge the purpose behind the action — whether it was to buy without advancing the price, or to force the price up, or to mark it down, or to discourage buying or selling by others, as the case might be. Not all transactions (on the tape) were significant, but the interpreter must detect those that were. He must see that one indicated a purpose. Someone or some group was carrying or attempting to carry something through. He must take advantage of that.

Tape reading of commodity prices was hampered by the lack of intraday volume until computers began calculating tick volume for any desired time period. Today, the tape reader who uses the right hardware can have 5-minute or 60-minute bar charts with tick volume for interpreting the ongoing struggle between buyers and sellers. Tick volume represents trading activity — that is, how many times prices change in a given time period, not how many contracts are traded.

There is no difference between judging market action on an intraday basis or on daily, weekly, and monthly charts except for the frequency of trading opportunities. Wyckoff wrote in *Studies in Tape Reading* (1910) that "it is unimportant whether you are endeavoring to forecast the next small half-hourly swing or the trend for the next two or three weeks. The same indications as to price, volume, activity, support, and pressure are exhibited in the preparation for both."

As a bond trader, I maintain 45-minute bar charts (with 45-minute tick volume) and use Wyckoff's techniques for capitalizing on price swings that usually cover several days. For day-trading purposes, a smaller time period is required. The following discussion deals with actual trading situations in June '82 bonds over a 30-day period.

Figure 1.1 shows the 45-minute price ranges from March

23 through April 7.

Although the larger picture is not a primary concern for tape reading, previous resistance and support levels are kept in mind. In this case, June '82 bonds had bottomed in September 1981 at 56-08. The first rally topped in November at 66-23 and a retest of the low ended in February 1982 at 57-10.

From the February bottom, prices advanced to 64-08 (the underside of the November top area) and a trading range formed between 64-08 and 61-08. Figure 1.1 picks up with a decline from the March 23rd high (63-28) within this trading range.

For the purpose of this study, let's assume that today is April 7, 1982, and we are reviewing the volume/price behavior for clues about the future direction of June bonds. Here are some observations about what has taken place:

1. Point #1 is a selling climax, as volume was heavier there than at any time within the decline from 63-28. Bonds closed in the middle of the range, indicating that buying was present.

2. After a two-day lateral movement, prices make new lows but reverse at point #2, negating much of the recent weakness. The market is in position to spring upward. (A spring occurs when prices decline below a support level and then reverse. If the next pullback holds above the low of the reversal and volume contracts, then the spring has been tested and prices should rally vigorously. If the response is weak, the spring will probably fail.)

3. Prices return to the minor trading range, and there is no volume on the pullback to #3. The range between the high and low is narrow at #3, indicating the market's unwillingness or inability to move lower. Bonds are on the springboard for a fast rally — an excellent place to go long and protect with a stop below the reversal.

FIGURE 1.1

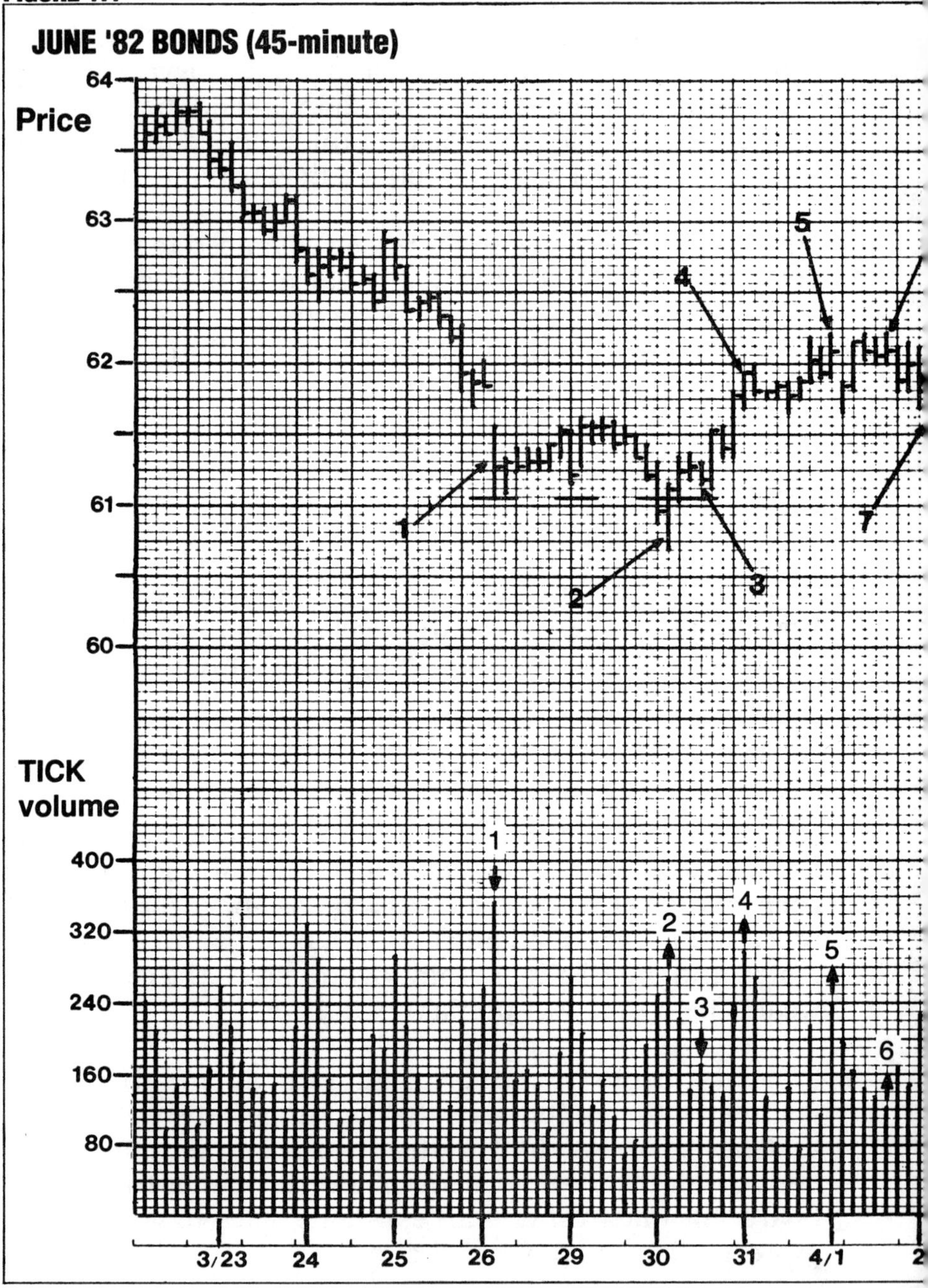
JUNE '82 BONDS (45-minute)
Price
64
63
62
61
60
TICK volume
400
320
240
160
80
1
2
3
4
5
6
7
3/23
24
25
26
29
30
31
4/1

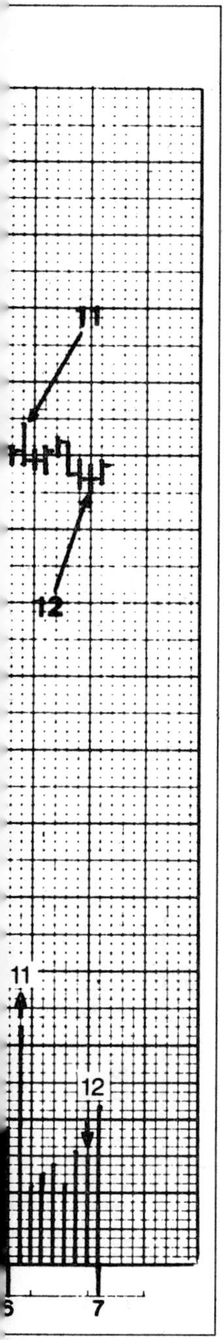

Figure 1.1
A look at the bond futures market with Wyckoff volume/price behavior method. Point 1 is a selling climax, point 2 is a spring, at point 3 bonds are on a springboard, and point 4 witnesses heavy demand due to the increasing volume. Point 5 indicates supply is appearing. Low volume at point 6 indicates that demand is tiring. Supply is entering the market, indicated by the increasing volume at point 7. The lack of increasing volume on the rally to point 8 is a negative sign. The sudden drop to point 9 shows that the sellers are in control. The lack of increasing volume at point 10 was a positive sign. The weak close at point 11 calls for another test of the lows. Volume dies down at point 12, forewarning of a rally.

FIGURE 1.2

JUNE '82 BONDS (4x12 point & figure chart)

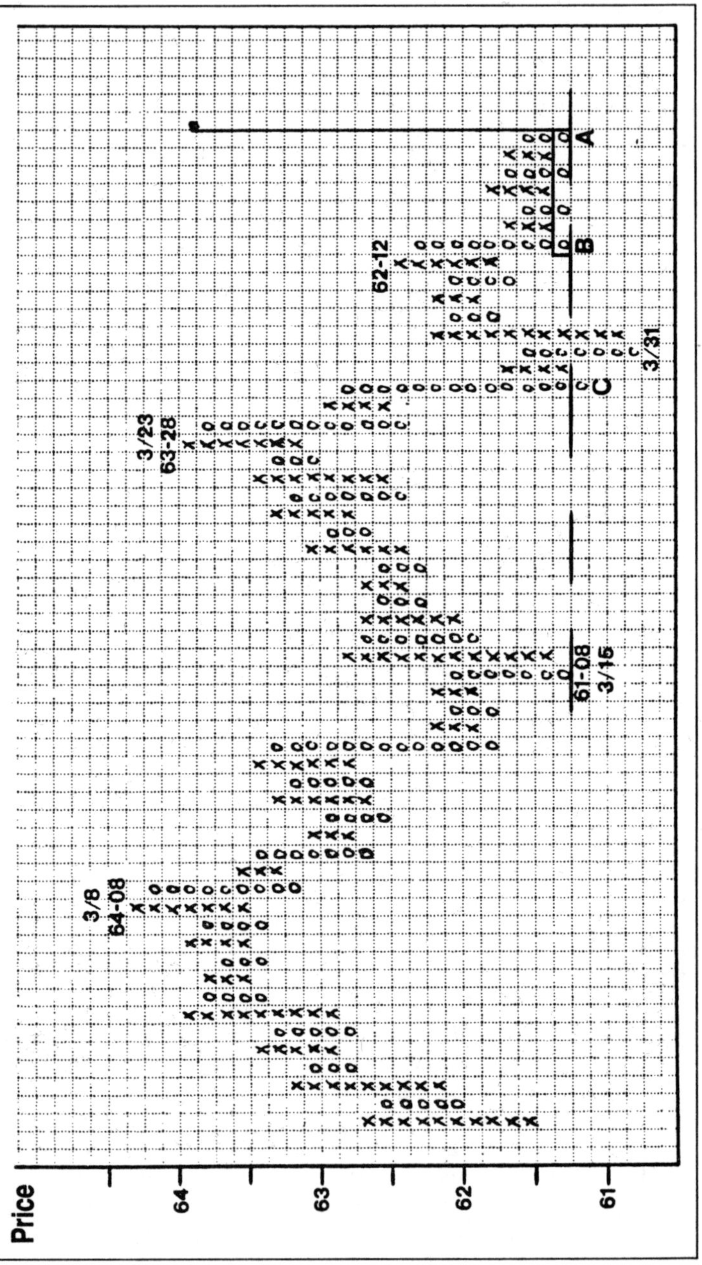

This point & figure chart uses X's for rallies and O's for declines. A 4x12 figure chart for the bond futures contract uses 4/32nds as a box size and a minimum of 12/32nds as a reversal.

4. Demand is present on the rally to #4 as volume is heavy. But at #5, demand meets resistance because the market is unable to make much headway despite the effort. Demand tires at #6.

5. Supply is evident on the break at #7 as volume increases sharply. However, the longs make one last effort to force prices higher on the rally to 62-12 at #8. Volume does not expand on this rally; notice how bonds give ground on the closings. The force of demand is weak.

6. The latest gains are quickly erased, trapping the weak longs who bought the breakout at #8. The sellers are in control at #9. Bonds try to recover but the resistance at 61-24 is overwhelming.

7. At #10, the market penetrates 61-08 and is poised to retest the March low. The inability of volume to increase on this breakdown would raise suspicions about the strength of the selling. But some indication of demand is needed before we will know that the downwave is ending.

8. Demand re-enters the market on the rally to #11, as revealed by the increase in volume and magnitude of the recovery. The poor closing at #11 shows that selling is still present at the 61-24 resistance level.

9. Prices slowly retreat without any sign of renewed selling pressure. In the area of #12, bonds close for three consecutive time periods within a 2/32 range. The force of the selling has died. The bond market on April 7 is at one of those "critical points" that Wyckoff described years ago:

> Successful tape reading is a study of force; it requires ability to judge which side has the greatest force behind it. One must have the courage to go with that side. There are critical points which occur in each swing...At these junctures it seems as though a feather's weight on either side would determine the

immediate trend. Anyone who can spot these points has much to win and little to lose, for he can always play with a stop placed close behind the turning point.

MARKET MANIPULATORS IN ACTION

We have observed the details of an eight-day trading range. As prices unfolded, the evidence mounted — with an occasional tinge of uncertainty — that some large interest was accumulating bonds. In retrospect, we can reconstruct their operations.

At #1, these large traders are taking profits on short positions under the cover of a selling panic created by longs scrambling to liquidate. During the two-day period from #1, the operators began buying. To find out how much more supply was around, they pressed the market lower to #2. We cannot know for sure, but perhaps they even made a public display of bearishness in the bond pit on this drive downward.

When their efforts failed to generate another onslaught of selling, the operators quickly covered all shorts and bought aggressively, causing the fast spring action from #3 to #4. At #5, they began taking profits, and the high volume at #7 signaled that they were attempting to push prices lower for the purpose of buying more bonds.

On the rally to #8, they withdrew their offerings to observe if demand was coming in from another quarter. Nothing significant happened, so they began pressing the market and probably with great fanfare. The floor monitors for the brokerage houses reported that well-known, large traders were selling; clients were notified and more selling entered the market on the decline to #9. When the volume of selling diminished at #10, the operators began covering shorts and going long on the rally to #11. They quietly bought more on the slow correction to #12.

All the evidence points to an upswing in bonds. The tape reader would immediately go long and place a protective sell stop below #10. The risk on the trade is 6/32nds.

Wyckoff relied on point and figure charts to measure how

far prices can move out of a congestion area. For this study, I have included a 4 x 12 point and figure chart (Figure 2.2). Each block equals 4/32nds, and reversals of 12/32nds or more are plotted. This chart shows the trading range that developed from the March 1982 high at 64-08.

It is appropriate to view the downwave to the March 31st low and recovery to 62-12 as the beginning of a spring. The pullback from 62-12 tested the spring, and a fast upmove should follow. Counting across the 61-08 line, the tight congestion between points A and B projects a conservative target of 63-28, which equals the March 23rd high. The larger objective is 66-28, based on the distance from A to C. A tape reader focuses on the conservative objective and remains alert for volume/price behavior that warns of another shift in trend. In the next chapter, we will see the markup in June '82 bonds and a new distribution phase.

2

Anatomy of a Market Move

To continue with our study of the June '82 bond market, next we'll dissect the volume/price behavior during the markup and distribution phase that evolved over a 13-day period.

In the last chapter, we established that large operators were accumulating bonds at point #12 prior to an upswing (Figure 2.1). The conservative point-and-figure count AB (Figure 2.2) indicated potential for a move to 63-28. Long positions were recommended for the opening on April 8, with protective sell stops placed beneath the low at #10.

Now let's look at the 13-day period during which the markup and distribution phase evolved:

April 8. June bonds open at 61-11 before moving to a low of 61-09. Based on an entry price of 61-11, we are risking 7/32nds for a gain of at least 2-1/2 points. After opening lower, prices steadily moved higher throughout the session. It is noteworthy to mention here that tick volume has a U-shaped pattern. Tick volume is heavy in the opening 45 minutes and tapers off toward midday. From this lull in activity, trading increases until the final rush of volume in the closing hour.

Whenever the volume at midday is heavier than at the opening, traders should be alert because something significant is usually happening. On April 8, the midday tick volume at #13 is heavier than on the opening. This occurs as the bond market breaks through the resistance at 62-12. Demand has overcome supply and the markup stage is in full gear. In the last 90 minutes, there is the usual profit taking, but the market refuses to give ground.

April 12. Bonds gap higher to #14. Volume is again heavy, but there is no influx of selling on the subsequent correction. At #15, June bonds trade for 45 minutes in a 4/32nd range, suggesting the pressure is off. By the end of the session, prices close on a firm note at 63-17.

April 13. On the opening at #16, June bonds rally to 63-27, thereby fulfilling the conservative point and figure objective. Volume on the opening is heavier than at any point in the uptrend and appears climactic. Prices close well off the high as operators are taking profits. This sequence of behavior tells the tape reader to take profits or at least raise sell stops to 63-12 (beneath the low of the opening time period). Prices hold for several hours, but the re-test of 63-27 fails to generate another upwave. Volume is not increasing, which suggests demand is tired. The market forms a small apex as the forces of supply and demand reach a temporary point of equilibrium.

At #17, the range is narrow and volume contracts. Prices must rally immediately or the sellers will have the upper hand. The tape reader would raise the sell stop to beneath the low at #17. If the trader is aggressive, a break would warrant a short position with buy stops placed at 63-28. The market moves downward off its hinge as supply overcomes demand.

April 14. The market opens lower at #18 but finds support as prices close on the high of the period. Volume is the heaviest since prices topped at #16, suggesting a minor selling climax has occurred. There is little or no followthrough on the upside, as prices stay close to the low of the opening time period. In the last 45 minutes at #19, the bond market penetrates the opening support level but closes well off the low. If the sellers are in control, the market should open lower on the next day.

April 15. Instead of continuing lower, prices rally on the opening at #20 and volume is heavier than at any point in the correction from #16. Demand has asserted itself, again putting bonds in a spring position. This opening rally was met with selling as prices closed off the high. If the next pullback is on light volume and holds above the low at #19, we will know the market is about to spring upward.

At #21, the market is on the springboard. The behavior is ideal: a narrow range, the lightest volume in days, and prices close in midrange. There is no more selling pressure. (Compare the behavior from #18 to #21 with the price action from #1 to #3.) Any existing short position must be covered at once (netting a half-point gain) and longs established; stops are placed 1/32nd below #19. On the point and figure chart, the congestion along the 62-28 line (DD) projects a minimum target of 64-12; the maximum objective is 65-04. From #21, bonds steadily move higher without attracting supply.

April 16. The bond market moves unobtrusively upward until the burst of activity on the closing. Prices reach 64-13, the first point and figure objective; volume is heavier than at any time since the low at #1. While there is no evidence of topping action, this behavior is an indication that large operators are unloading part of their long position on strength. Stops on long positions should be raised to 63-15.

April 19. On the opening at #22, bonds drop more than in any time period since the rally from #10; volume is as heavy as on the previous day's closing. This is more evidence that large interests are taking profits.

In the second time period, the selling ceases. Notice that the resistance line across the high at #16 serves as support. With the absence of selling, bonds rush to new highs at #23. Volume expands on the rally and contracts on the pullback. At the close at #24, the buyers make a large effort to push the market higher, as indicated by the increase in volume.

FIGURE 2.1

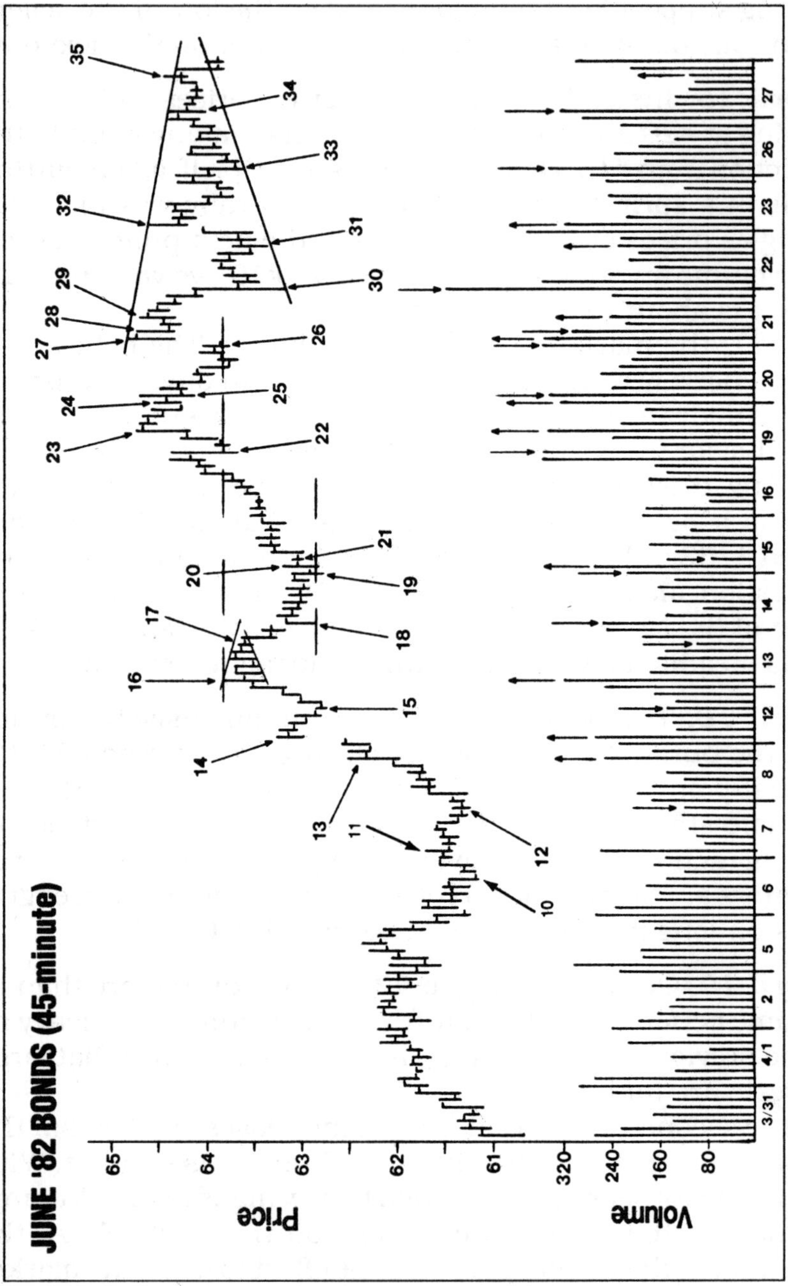

This chart is a 45-minute vertical bar chart of the bond futures contract. At the bottom is a tick volume chart, which indicates the number of times the price changed during each 45 minutes, not the number of contracts that traded at each price level.

April 20. In the first 45 minutes, at #25, bonds open higher, encounter resistance against the previous day's high, and reverse downward. The heavy volume on the decline adds to the bearish picture that is forming. The tape reader would take profits on long positions. A short position also could be established, with buy stops placed 1/32nd above the high at #25.

Bonds decline into the area of previous support at #22 and on top of the previous resistance line. The lack of volume on this decline warns the tape reader to take profits on any shorts at the close. The heavy volume on the close suggests that other traders have spotted the weakness in bonds and are selling the market. Since prices gave little ground in the last 45 minutes, we can assume the operators are supporting the market in order to build a larger short position. Another test of the high is possible.

April 21. The market opens strong and makes a new high at #27. If the uptrend is to remain intact, there must be followthrough. Instead, at #28, bonds sell off and volume remains heavy. This is bearish behavior, and the light volume rally at #29 indicates demand is tiring.

Looking across the chart from #29, we can see that bonds have persistently met supply around the 64-24 level (#23, #25, #27, #28). For all the effort to move higher, the rally to #27 exceeded the previous high by only 3/32nds. This represents shortening of the upward movement and an upthrust (the opposite of a spring). The heavy selling at #28 quickly negated the move to new highs.

With this bearish behavior and the tired rally at #29, a short position is warranted. Buy stops are placed 2/32nds above the high at #27. The bond market begins to slide lower until the collapse in the last time period at #30. Given the bearish behavior that preceded it, the fall at #30 is a major sign of weakness and not a washout. It indicates that sellers have gained the upper hand.

April 22. Bonds open unchanged and make a lackluster attempt to rally. On the pullback to #31, there is no evidence

FIGURE 2.2

JUNE '82 BONDS (4/12 point & figure)

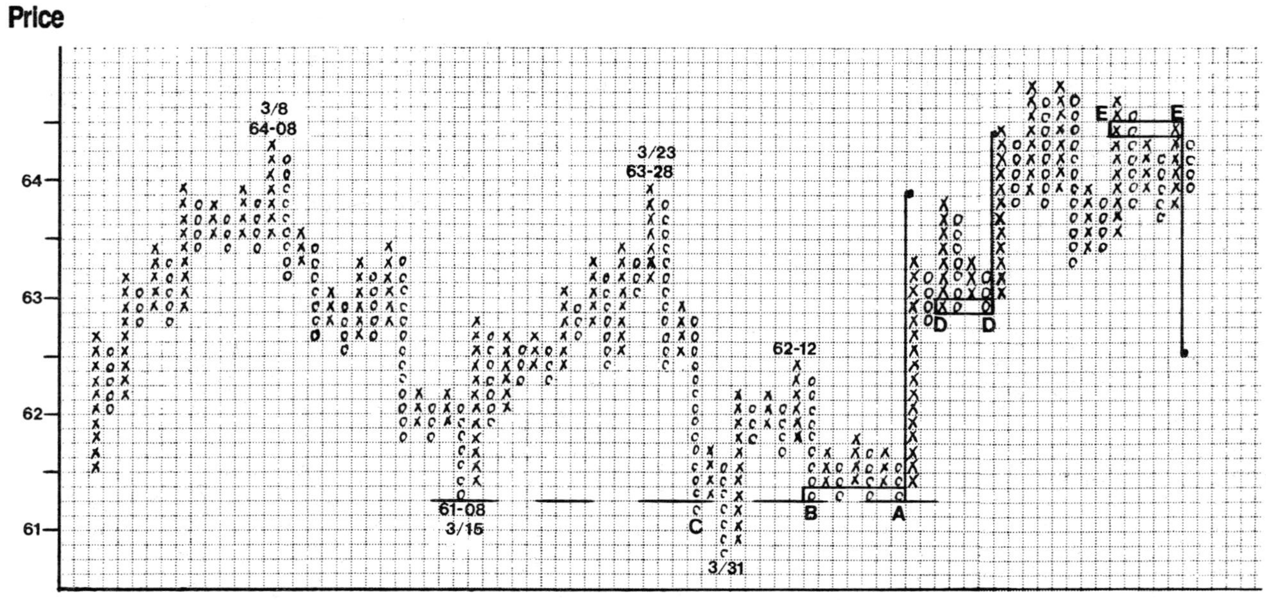

The point & figure chart of the bond futures contract uses a 4/32nds price-per-box label and a 12/32nds reversal. This means the market must move at least 12/32nds for the trend to be considered reversed. During advances X's are plotted and during declines O's are plotted.

of selling pressure; therefore, the tape reader takes profits on the short position. Bonds rally on the close as the sellers have backed off.

April 23. The market makes another surge toward the highs on the opening at #32; however, it is met by new selling as prices end the time period on the low. By the end of the day, all the opening gains are erased as the bonds close unchanged. The sign of weakness still looms heavily on the tape reader's mind, but there is no evidence that the downtrend is ready to resume.

April 26. Bonds open lower at #33 as the sellers make a strong effort to break the market. However, the minor uptrend line drawn across #30 and #31 checks the decline. Prices rally away from the danger point and push higher on the close. The closing rally stops against a downtrend line drawn across the tops at #27 and #32. It is obvious now that an apex is forming, but on a larger scale than experienced at #17.

April 27. Again, the market opens lower at #34 on heavy volume. Prices manage to close off the low of this time period as demand is still present. During the next three time periods, the price ranges narrow and volume dries up. The bond market is in position to rally out of the apex. The force of the demand will tell whether buyers have gained the upper hand in this struggle.

At #35, the bond market moves slightly above the apex and the previous day's high. Volume remains light and prices close unchanged for the time period. The tape reader recognized that demand is exhausted. Counting only a portion of the top along the 64-12 line (EE on the point and figure chart), the reader projects a conservative objective of 62-16. Short positions are established and stops placed 1/32nd above the high at #32.

On the next time period, volume is heavy as bonds fall beneath the low of the day. The distribution phase is complete. June bonds declined to 62-15 on May 4.

From the beginning of the upwave (#10) to the conclusion of the distribution phase (#35), we have concentrated only on his pronouncements about the future of interest rates. We considered none of this information. The trader who isolates himself from everything but the market and takes the time to study what the market is saying about itself can duplicate the trading techniques developed 80 years ago by Richard Wyckoff.

PART III

The Wyckoff Method: Five Steps to Success

by Craig F. Schroeder

1
Determining Trend

The Wyckoff method as it is taught today represents the results of more than 100 years of continuous market study. Those years have brought the development of numerous refinements and a variety of applications. The basic building blocks of the approach, however, have remained the same. The ability to stand the test of time in a field where techniques come and go as regularly as the seasons makes a working knowledge of the method a worthwhile undertaking for all serious investors and speculators.

In his course in stock market science and technique, Richard Wyckoff stated the basics of his method in five steps. These five building blocks are as follows:

Step 1: Determine the present position and probable future trend of the market. Then decide how you are going to play the game: long, short or neutral.

Step 2: Select from those stocks in harmony with the market the ones stronger than the market in a bull market. In a bear market, select those that are weaker than the market.

Step 3: Select those stocks that have built up a cause, a potential count for a move in keeping with your goals.

Step 4: Determine each stock's readiness to move. Analyze the vertical and figure charts of the candidates with the help of the buying and selling tests.

Step 5: Time your commitments with a turn in the market.

The five steps of the Wyckoff method can be divided into three groups that ask and help answer three important questions. Step 1 stands alone and asks the question *what*. Steps 2 through 4 can be grouped together and ask the question *who*. Step 5 stands alone and asks the question *when*. Therefore, by employing all five steps, the investor or speculator can determine what type of market operation to undertake, which individual stocks or bonds represent the best candidate(s) and when the best time is to make a commitment. Correct answers to all three questions put the odds of success decisively in favor of the investor. Two correct answers still give the investor good odds for success. Even one correct answer can at least prevent a disaster.

IDENTIFYING THE TREND

Determining the present position of the market requires that a determination as to the present trend of the market be made as well. Wyckoff analysis dictates that the trend of the market is either up, down or neutral (trading range). It also specifies that the market trades in three trends at any given time. There is a short-term trend, an intermediate trend and a long-term trend. There is no set rule as to the amount of time that each trend includes. An intraday trader of futures or options may wish to define a short-term trend as one that begins, unfolds and ends all in the same day. For this trader, an intermediate trend can be completed in several days and a long-term trend can be completed in a few weeks. A long-term investor in government bonds would be likely to define the three trends very differently. For this individual, a short-term trend will frequently begin, unfold and end over a period of several weeks. A long-term trend can last a year or more.

Each investor or speculator needs to make an objective decision as to the best trend definition for his or her situation. Many individuals needlessly turn the odds of success against them at this point without having placed a single buy or sell order. Defining trends that are too short term in nature is the biggest single error. A shorter-term operation results in higher expenses and requires more time. It is also more difficult because the windows of opportunity in which trades need to be executed to be profitable are smaller. Therefore, the individual who lacks the experience, the time or the resources but chooses to follow a short-term path anyway is not likely to succeed.

Wyckoff analysis defines uptrends using a demand line and an overbought line. A downtrend is defined by a supply line and an oversold line. A trading range is defined by a support level and a resistance level. Figure 1.1 shows an example of a shorter-term downtrend using points 1 and 3 to define the supply line and point 2 to define the oversold line parallel to the supply line. Figure 1.2 shows an intermediate uptrend defined by lines CC and DD. It also shows an example of a longer-term uptrend defined by lines EE and FF. The mechanics of how these lines are defined and the variations that can be justified is a subject for a separate discussion. For now, all that is needed are examples to illustrate how the position in the current trend influences the probable future trend.

BUCKING THE TREND

Once a trend has been defined, the market will continue to trade within it until supply and demand factors change sufficiently to break the trend. The short-term trend defined in Figure 1.1 is most likely to continue if the market is positioned near the supply line. Since the line of least resistance has already been defined as being down, a position near the supply line provides the market with the greatest amount of distance in which to make additional downside progress before the support provided by the oversold line is reached. Therefore, if

FIGURE 1.1

Shorter-term downtrend

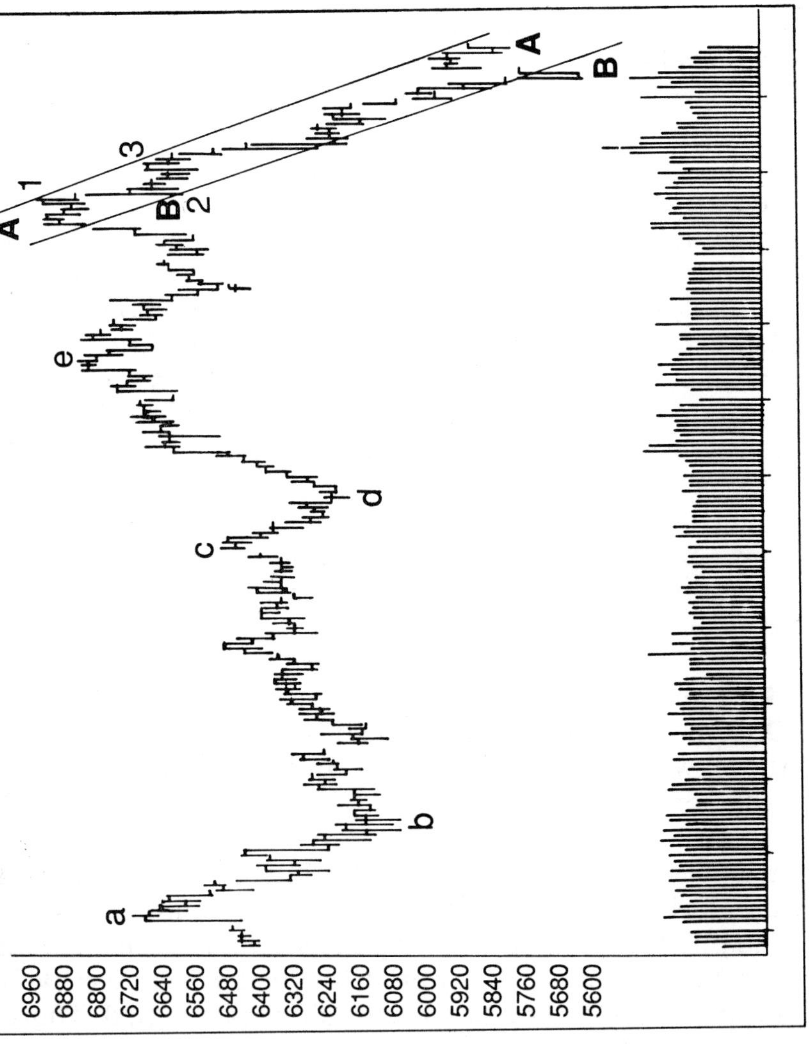

The daily bar chart of the Wyckoff wave has a downtrend channel drawn on it. Line AA defines a supply line, while line BB is labeled as the oversold line. Short positions should be placed near the supply line. The position then offers the greatest amount of distance for downside progress.

the market is positioned near the supply line and volume factors provide confirmation, it may be concluded that the probable future trend is also likely to be down. Consequently, action on the short side should be considered.

As the market approaches and reaches the oversold line of the downtrend in Figure 1.1, the probable future trend becomes more doubtful. This is because the oversold line provides support, which can lead to a rally that may break the trend. If the trend is broken, the future trend may be a new downtrend, a trading range or an uptrend. Therefore, the uncertainty over the direction of the future trend discourages new action. If the market does rally away from the oversold line, it may meet supply again as it approaches the supply line. If so, the probable future trend is likely to be down and new action on the short side may be considered again.

In an uptrend such as the one defined by lines CC and DD in Figure 1.2, the situation is reversed. The uptrend that is defined by these lines is most likely to be the future trend as well if the market is positioned near the demand line. In this case, the line of least resistance is already pointed in an upward direction. Therefore, a position near the demand line provides the market with the greatest amount of room in which to make additional upside progress. Thus, action on the long side should be considered. As the market rallies in the trend and approaches the overbought line, the resistance provided by that line is increasingly likely to stop upside progress. This results in greater uncertainty about the future trend, which in turn discourages new action on the long side.

If the current trend of the market is not up or down, it is neutral or a trading range. Depending on the market's position in the trading range, it can provide opportunities on both the long and short side of the market. In a trading range, the market as a whole makes little if any additional upside or downside progress. An established high provides resistance to upside progress and an established low provides support to downside progress. A trading range in the general market is caused by relatively rapid rotation among the individual stocks. As a result, some stocks will make substantial ad-

FIGURE 1.2

Intermediate uptrend

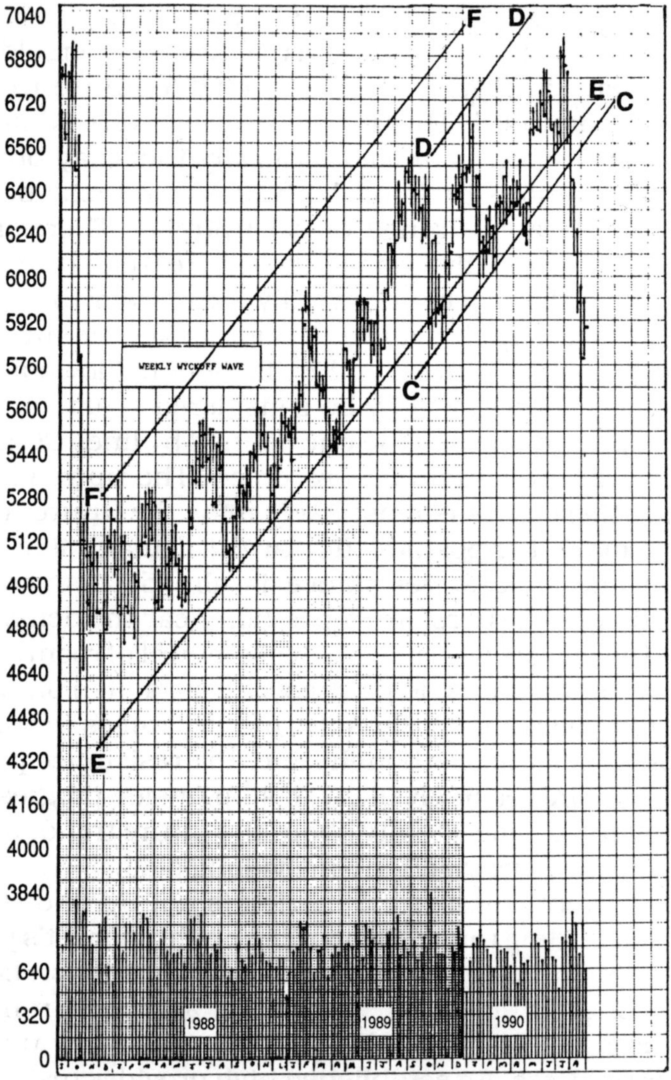

The weekly bar chart of the Wyckoff wave shows two uptrend channels. The long-term uptrend channel is defined by the demand line EE and the overbought line by FF. The intermediate channel is defined by the demand line CC and the overbought line by DD. Purchases should be made when the market is near the demand line. This position is with the trend and provides more opportunity during the advance.

vances as the market rallies in a trading range and others will make substantial declines as the market reacts. The process of rotation that occurs while the market is in a trading range results in opportunities on both the long side and the short side.

If the trend of the market is neutral, the probability of the future trend also being neutral increases as the market approaches and reaches either the support level or the resistance level, providing volume factors give the necessary confirmation. As the market is stopped by the resistance at the top of the trading range, those stocks, which have been relatively weak to the market during the rally that produces a position at the top of the trading range, are most likely to provide the best participation on the downside as the market moves toward the bottom of the trading range. Therefore, these issues should be considered for positions on the short side. At the bottom of the trading range, those issues that have been relatively strong to the market should provide the best participation to the upside as the market moves back toward the top of the range. Therefore, these issues should be considered for positions on the long side.

STAKING OUT A POSITION

At this point, it should be clear that a position within an established trend that is most likely to benefit from the continuation of the trend represents the best opportunity for the investor or speculator. There are positions within an established trend that suggest the likelihood of a change in the direction of the trend. The Wyckoff method also addresses these. However, these positions are more complex and go beyond the limited scope of the discussion here.

The points I have outlined as the best trading opportunities are all considered danger points. They are points at which price movement in the direction of the trend, or in the opposite direction if the trend is a trading range, must begin or the trend will be violated. On the surface, establishing a position at a danger point might appear to be a crazy idea. However, the points of greatest danger represent the points of minimum risk. This means that the position is established at a point at which the smallest amount of movement possible in the wrong direction will clearly indicate that an error in judgment has been made. If so, the investor or trader can eliminate the position, preserve as much of his or her initial capital as possible and move on to another potential opportunity. Preservation of capital should be a foremost objective. The best way to accomplish this is to cut losses short and let profits run.

THE WYCKOFF WAVE

To determine the current trend, the present position and probable future trend of the market, a means of charting the market's action to reveal the general direction of the trend is necessary. The general trend of the market is created by the interaction of the forces of supply and demand, which are reflected in the selling and buying pressures that cause stock prices to fluctuate. The total price movement is the general trend. The ideal approach to observing and measuring this movement is with a common stock price index. The Wyckoff Wave is such an index.

The Wyckoff wave is not simply an average of stock prices; it is an index that serves as a miniature version of the entire market. The wave is composed of the intraday movement of eight individual stocks. Currently, these eight issures are:

Bristol Myers (BMY)	**General Motors (GM)**
Dow Chemical (DOW)	**IBM (IBM)**
Exxon (XON)	**Merrill Lynch (MER)**
General Electric (GE)	**Union Pacific (UNP)**

These stocks are all market leaders and are widely held, actively traded and participate in most market moves.

2 Relative Strength and Weakness

The concept addressed in Step 2 of the Wyckoff method is relative strength and weakness:

Step 2: Select from those stocks in harmony with the market the ones stronger than the market in a bull market. In a bear market, select those that are weaker than the market.

In the last chapter I discussed step one, identifying the trend. If the analysis completed in step one indicates that the best course of action is a neutral position, then there is no need to continue to step two. However, if step 1's analysis indicates there is a trend, step two of the Wyckoff method may help identify the best individual issue(s) in which to establish a position.

Selecting candidates

Relative strength and weakness is an amazingly simple idea that is frequently overlooked by investors and speculators. A stock that is relatively strong to the market is likely to remain relatively strong unless or until there is enough of a change in the forces of supply and demand to alter the character of the action.

The concept of relative strength and weakness is useful in all three types of trends. In an uptrend, the relatively strong stocks represent the best candidates for long positions while the relatively weak stock represent the worst candidates. This is where many investors and speculators frequently make a potentially fatal error — the conclusion that the relatively weak stocks during an uptrend in the general market represent the biggest bargains and therefore, the best opportunities on the long side. This is generally not true. Stocks that are relatively weak during an uptrend in the general market are in that position for a reason. You cannot assume that the stocks have been overlooked by the large interests in the market.

It is much more likely that the reason involves poor fundamentals, which may or may not be public knowledge. If the uptrend in the general market is strong enough or lasts long enough, the process of rotation suggests that some of the relatively weak stocks will make meaningful upside progress. However, the odds do not favor these stocks catching up with or surpassing the relatively strong issues, which are the ones most responsible for defining and fueling the uptrend.

When the general market is in a downtrend, the relatively strong stocks represent the worst candidates for short positions while the relatively weak stocks represent the best candidates. A stock's lack of participation in the direction of the trend should not be looked at as an indication of excessive value. When the general market moves into a trading range, both the relatively weak stocks and the relatively strong stocks represent potential trading opportunities. The position of the market within the trading range determines whether the relatively strong stocks or the relatively weak stocks represent the best opportunities.

As the market approaches the resistance level at the top of the trading range, the stocks that are relatively weak represent the best opportunities on the short side in anticipation of a move back to the bottom of the trading range. These stocks do not have to be in trading ranges themselves. They are more likely to be in downtrends as a result of the relative weakness.

As the market approaches the bottom of the trading range, the relatively strong stocks represent the best opportunities on the long side in anticipation of a move back toward the top of the trading range. These stocks do not have to be in trading ranges. Their relative strength is likely to have them in uptrends.

MEASURING RELATIVE STRENGTH AND WEAKNESS

Relative strength and weakness is not a subjective concept. It can be measured in absolute terms. The easiest method involves identifying a series of important rally tops and reaction bottoms in the general market. In Figure 2.1, a series of tops and bottoms have been marked by a through g. After these points are identified, the percentage move from one point to the next is calculated. Between point a and point b, the Wyckoff wave declined 9.538%. Between points b and c it rallied 7.084%. The remaining measurements are as follows: c to d = -4.769%, d to e = +10.501%, e to f = -5.117% and f to g = +6.994%.

Similar measurements should be taken on all stocks that are being monitored on a regular basis. This can be a time-consuming process. If you are following a large number of stocks is being followed, you may wish to consider computerizing the process. If that is not feasible, consideration should be limited to the issues that make up the index that is being used to follow the course of the general market. An investor or speculator who uses the Wyckoff wave can limit his universe to eight stocks. An individual who follows the Dow Jones Industrial Average (DJIA) should consider the performance of all 30 of its components. You do not have to follow hundreds of stocks to realize an above-average return from the market.

The individual who is playing the shorter-term moves in the market is most interested in the move that immediately follows point g. Therefore, the relative performances on the moves from e to f and f to g are illuminating. Forecasting a reaction

FIGURE 2.1

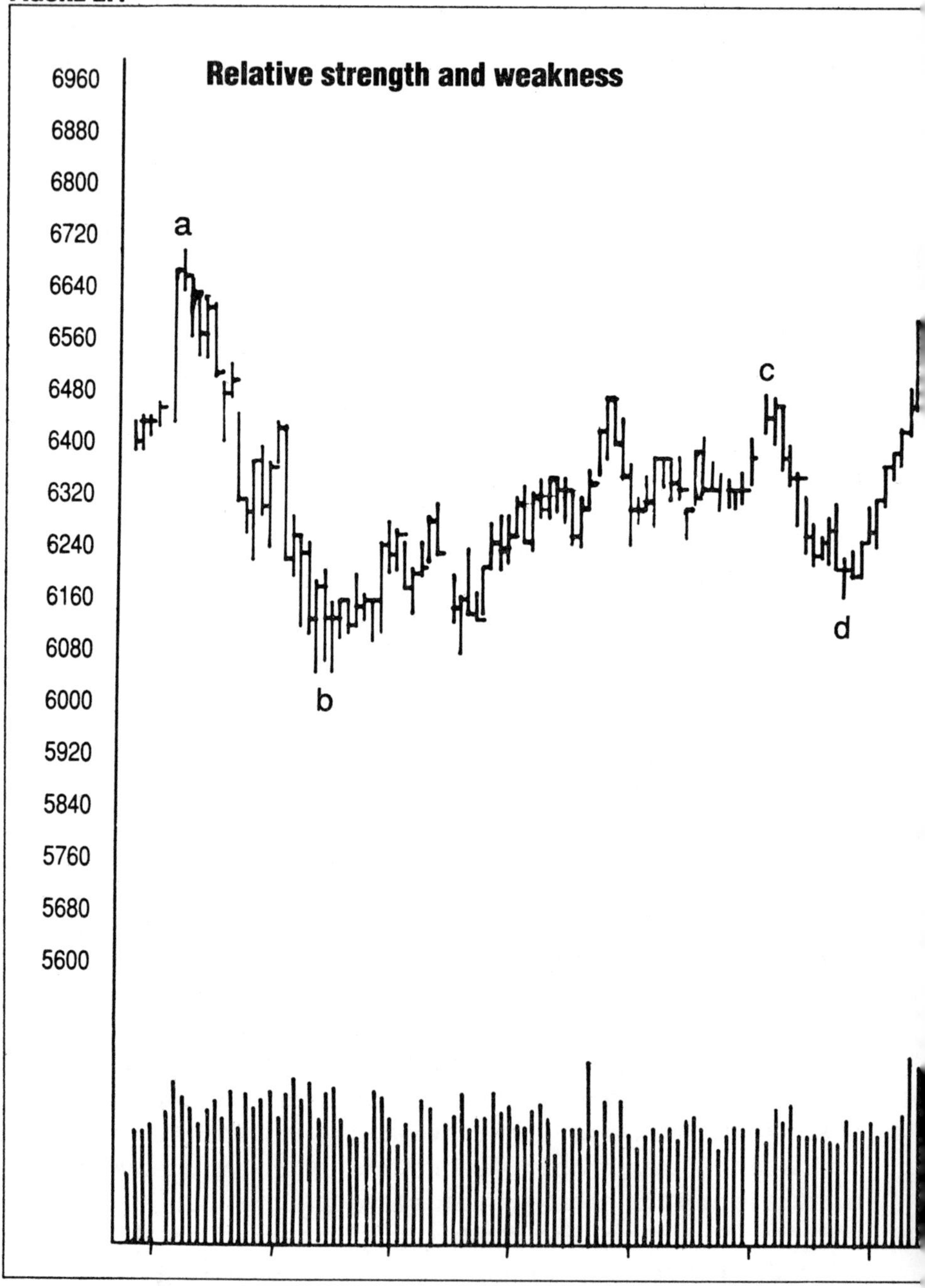
Relative strength and weakness
6960
6880
6800
6720
6640
6560
6480
6400
6320
6240
6160
6080
6000
5920
5840
5760
5680
5600
a
b
c
d

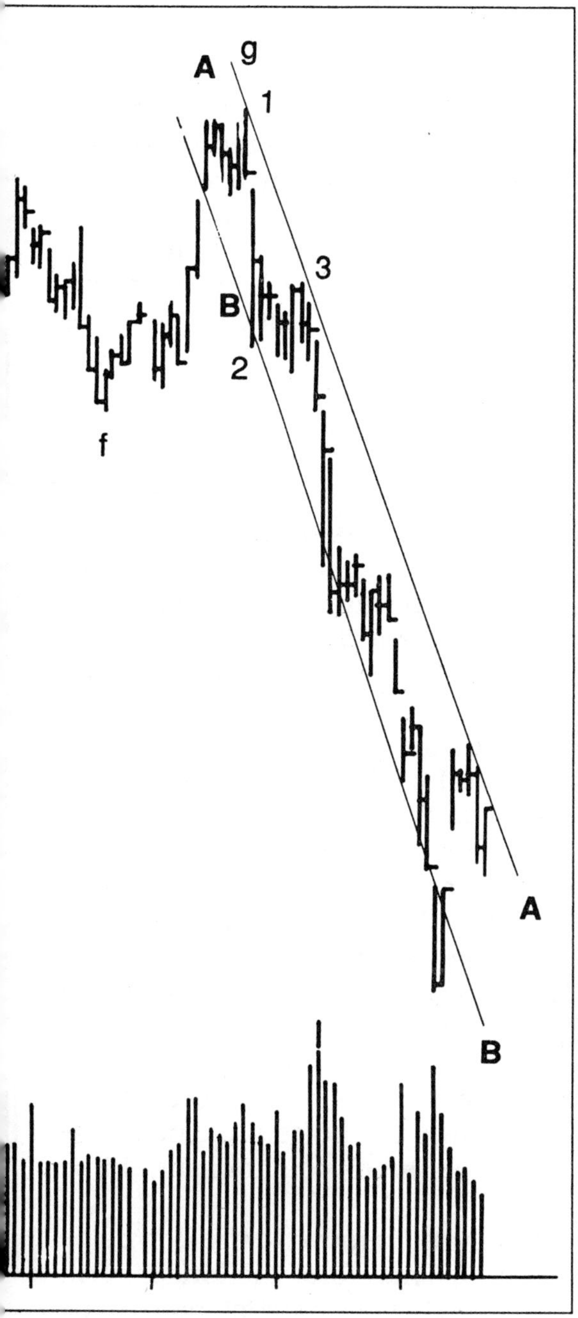

Relative strength and weakness can be measured by identifying a series of important rally tops and reaction bottoms in the general market, marked a through g, and then calculating the percentage move from one point to the next. Between point a and b, the Wyckoff wave declined 9.538%. Between points b and c it rallied 7.084%.

following point g, stocks that are weaker than the market on the move from e to f and from f to g represent the best candidates for short positions.

As the trading perspective of the individual expands, the number of reactions and rallies that are considered should be increased. This helps avoid being influenced by a short-term move that is not consistent with the action overall. An intermediate investor should consider adding the action from c to d and d to e to determine which stocks are the strongest and weakest. The longer-term investor should consider adding the moves from a to b and b to c as well. The stocks that most consistently outperform the general market in a manner consistent with the type of position that is anticipated represent the best opportunities.

If no stock outperforms the market on every move, the ones that outperform the market on the greatest number of moves represent the best opportunities. In these cases, the most recent rallies and reactions should be given more weight.

In Figure 2.1, the longer-term perspective indicated by the action from point a to point g suggests that the market is in a trading range due to very little upside progress being made during the period. An investor trading the market from this perspective and viewing the trend of the market as being a trading range can justify action on the short side at point g in anticipation of a move back toward the bottom of the range. However, an intermediate investor viewing the market from c to g sees it as being in an uptrend. A reaction may still be anticipated, but attempting to participate in it is difficult to justify because the anticipated move is contrary to the direction of the trend. The shorter-term speculator viewing the market from point e to point g and seeing virtually no upside progress may conclude that the market has moved into a trading range. A move back toward the bottom of the range may be anticipated and selecting a stock to short should be considered.

Figure 2.1 clearly indicates that the move to the downside following point g was substantial. Therefore, the longer-term and shorter-term players in the market who participated in the anticipated reaction realized a substantial reward. The intermediate-term player, however, is left out.

The Wyckoff method is not magic. It does not guarantee the investor or speculator that he will be correct 100% of the time. It should be noted, however, that in this case an error in judgment resulted in a lost opportunity, but the dollar cost was zero. Other errors may result in actual losses, but other aspects of the Wyckoff method address techniques for limiting losses.

After applying the first two steps of the Wyckoff method to a particular market situation, the investor or speculator knows which side of the market to consider playing. Ranking stocks by relative performance compared to an index produces a list of candidates for trading. However, it is likely that the screening provided by the second step in the Wyckoff method will leave more potential candidates than the available funds can accommodate. Steps three and four of the Wyckoff method continue and complete the stock selection process, looking at how far potential candidates are likely to move and how soon.

Those two additional criteria, when combined with relative strength and weakness considerations, should result in a manageable group of candidates with an above-average likelihood of producing a worthwhile return.

3
Identifying Opportunities

Completing the first two steps of the Wyckoff method provides the investor or speculator with information that is essential for success. At this point, he or she knows whether to consider establishing long positions for an anticipated advance or short positions for a projected decline. In addition, he has a group of candidates from which to select the issues in which positions will be established. The next two steps of the Wyckoff method provide the basis for identifying the best opportunities from among the group of potential candidates.

CAUSE AND SELECT

Step 3 of the Wyckoff method involves selecting those stocks that have built up a cause in keeping with your goals. Many aspects of the Wyckoff approach employ the concept of cause and effect. In this step, the concept is applied using a point & figure chart. A cause on a point & figure chart is identified as a horizontal buildup of postings that develops at one particular level or over a relatively narrow range while the stock or the market as a whole is in a trading range. The cause is measured by the number of divisions that it covers on the point & figure

FIGURE 3.1

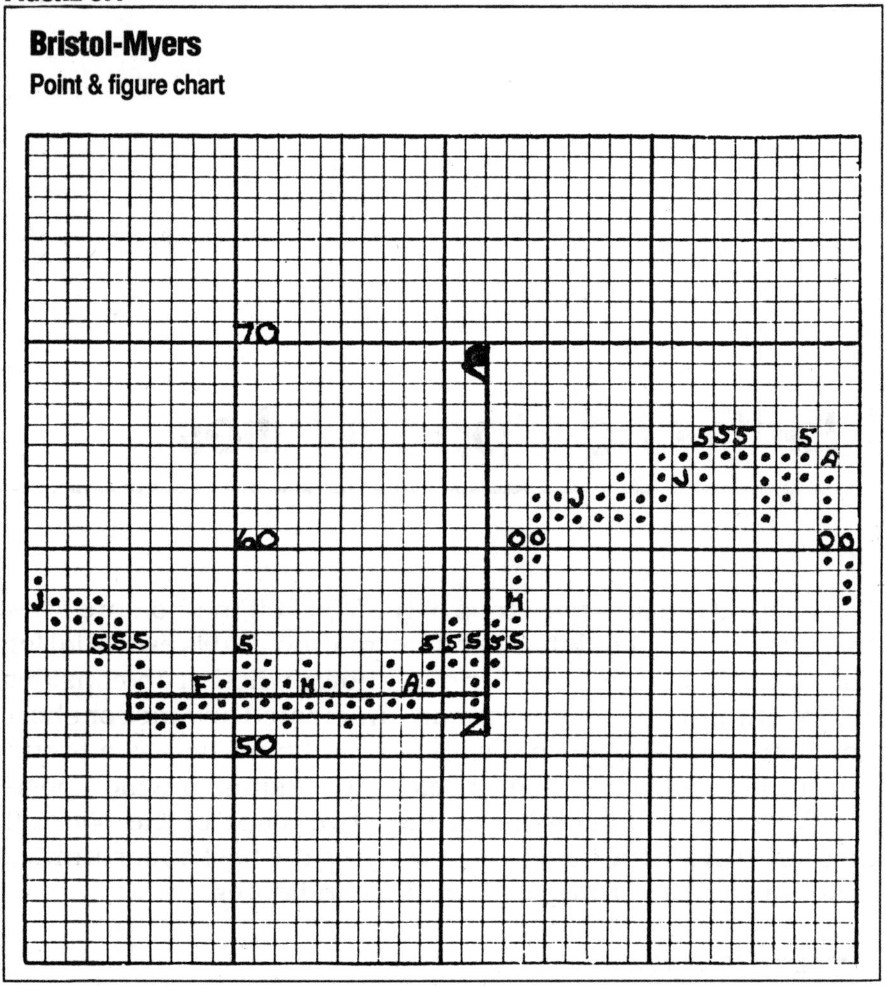

In this point & figure chart of Bristol-Myers, the 52-level is selected as the level at which to measure the potential move because it represents the bottom of the last reaction.

chart. Figure 3.1, which is a point & figure chart of Bristol-Myers, shows a cause at the 52 level.

The chart of Bristol-Myers begins on January 1, 1990. It shows that a trading range developed in January and lasted until April. During this period, the stock traded in a range from a low of approximately 51 to a high of approximately 55. The

52 level is selected as the level at which to measure the potential because it represents the bottom of the last reaction before the stock broke out of the trading range to the upside. Measuring from right to left, the trading range occupies 17 divisions on the chart. Therefore, the stock is said to have a count of 17 points at the 52 level, which represents its cause or potential. The 17-point horizontal cause indicates the likelihood of a 17-point vertical effect. In this case, the 17-point potential cause is added to the level at which it is measured and to the low point of the trading range, resulting in an objective range of 68 to 69. The stock's own action is indicating the possibility of a move to the 68 or 69 level, which is equal to about 33% of the value at the count level.

Why should there be a relationship between the length of time that a stock takes to move sideways and the possibility of an upside or downside price target if the stock moves out of the trading range? The theory is that as a stock moves in a sideways fashion, traders and investors build up a certain passiveness or apathy toward the stock. Typically, in such a situation, the current "fundamentals" relating to the stock value may be widely known; in effect, the stock may simply be lacking a following of sorts. Over the course of time, however, many factors can change, directly or indirectly affecting the value of the stock. The strength of the economy, the management of the company involved, or any number of events could suddenly change investors' attitudes. If a stock has been trading sideways for a long time there may have been a buildup of ownership by "strong hands" able to detect some very positive developments afoot in the company, which could change investors' attitudes toward the stock. While the stock was moving sideways the "strong hands" may have been able to accumulate large holdings, and once a rally is underway, the savvy investors would not be willing to sell their shares until prices were much higher. By observing the length of time that the stock takes to move sideways, a trader can deduce the potential move for the stock.

Each stock that is a potential candidate for a position should have its count or potential measured and its objective range determined. Those stocks with the biggest counts have the greatest potential and should represent the best candidates in which to establish positions. How much potential is enough is up to the investor. If a substantial number of stocks are still being considered at the completion of step 2, it is best to insist that a stock have a count that indicates a substantial potential. Using a potential of at least 50%, for example, will help reduce the number of candidates.

When determining which stocks have the greatest potential, be sure to measure each stock in question from the current level to the objective. If Bristol-Myers is at 52 when the potential is measured, a 30% advance is indicated. However, if it is already at 60, the potential remaining from the count at the 52 level is only 13%. Those stocks that are the strongest or the weakest are least likely to be in trading ranges, and they are the most likely to have left their count levels far behind. As a result, their remaining potential may not measure up to the requirement determined by the investor. Sometimes, the best candidates determined by steps 1 and 2 of the Wyckoff method will be the worst candidates indicated by step 3. The investor should therefore limit his further consideration to those that meet his minimum potential requirement, thus weeding out the possibles even further.

A student of the Wyckoff method should never forget that point & figure charts provide indications only. Holding to an objective indicated by figure charts even when the price and volume action suggests that the objective is not going to be reached invites disaster. As a result of changing supply and demand factors that develop after the potential has been put in place, but before it has been worked out, some stocks will overrun their indicated objectives while others will fall short. Those that fall short are most likely to produce problems for the investor.

JUDGING CHARACTER

Fortunately, certain aspects of the Wyckoff approach help an investor judge the character of the action. They can help determine whether a stock in which a position is held will or will not reach the objective; if not, the position can be closed out before paper profits are given back. For the investor who has not yet learned these finer points of the approach, or for the individual who chooses not to learn them, step 4 of the Wyckoff method provides the information required to utilize a simple risk-management device to help avoid a disaster. A student of the Wyckoff method always uses a stop order to limit loss or to protect a profit. The Wyckoff approach teaches the placement of stops using a profit risk ratio. Assume that BMY in Figure 3.1 is at the 52 level and that all considerations indicate that a position may be established at that level. The potential profit is to the 68 level, or 16 points. Sixteen points represents the profit side of the profit/risk ratio. Wyckoff theory states that the minimum acceptable profit risk ratio is 3 to 1. Therefore, if the anticipated profit is 16 points, the risk may be as much as 5-1/4 points without breaking the 3 to 1 guideline. The risk may be less, which will result in a higher profit/risk ratio, which in turn is better than a lower ratio. The stop, however, should always be placed below a previously defined support level.

Note that the potential in BMY for the low figure change during the trading range was 51, indicating that the stock traded at least as low as 51 but did not trade any lower than 50-1/8. Therefore, the initial stop order may be placed as high as 49-7/8 and still be below previously defined support. If the entry point is 52, the risk is 2-1/8 points. This risk, when combined with the potential profit of 16 points, results in a profit risk ratio of 16 to 2.1, which is better than 7 points of potential profit for each profit risk, an excellent profit/risk ratio. Assuming that this stock ranked highly from a relative strength standpoint, its substantial potential and excellent profit/risk ratio make it a good candidate of a position.

FINAL CONSIDERATIONS FOR DECISIONS

Upon completion of step 3 of the Wyckoff method, the investor knows most of what he needs to know to make an informed decision as to which stocks represent the best candidates of a position. At this point, he knows which stocks are outperforming the market and how much farther they are likely to move and how much may be risked to realize the anticipated profit. The investor is close to making a decision about taking a position. The final considerations determine each stock's readiness to move and the proximity of the general market to a turning point. These considerations are addressed in steps 4 and 5 of the Wyckoff method.

4
Buying and Selling Tests

The fourth step of the Richard Wyckoff method on stock market science and techniques, to review, is explained thus: *Determine each stock's readiness to move, then analyze the vertical line chart and figure chart of the candidates previously selected by the use of buying and selling tests.*

The first three steps of the Wyckoff method are simple and easy to apply. Step 4 can also be simply stated. Hidden behind the simplicity in this case, however, is a wide range of considerations to be addressed, most of which require the use of an element that is much less of a factor when applying any of the first three steps: good judgment, which must be developed through practice and cannot be learned from a book. What *can* be learned are tools that can aid in the development of good judgment. These are the focus of step 4 of the Wyckoff method.

READY OR NOT

Whether a stock is ready to move is determined by its current position compared with the previous action and the kind of action that has brought it there. With few exceptions, positions that appear ready to move occur at or near the completion of reactions or rallies. A stock will indicate a readiness to rise as it completes a reaction and it will indicate a readiness to drop as it completes a rally.

Though many finer points must be considered in the fourth step of the Wyckoff method, two principles can be put to work immediately in conjunction with Steps 1 through 3: position and nature of action.

The nature of the action, which is determined by relating price and volume action, is a good indicator of when direction is likely to change. Being able to read the character of the action will help in taking a position closer to the completion of a rally or reaction than would otherwise be possible.

When a stock is rallying, demand is in control; good quality or increasing demand will tend to keep the rally going. If applying the first three steps of the Wyckoff method have revealed the stock to be a potential short candidate, the object at this point is to determine when demand will lose control on a rally. The loss of control will coincide with the completion of the rally and the best time and place to take action on the short side.

During a rally, the presence and quality of demand are indicated by wider daily price spreads from the low to the high, increasing volume from day to day resulting in strong closes and increasing amounts of net upside progress from day to day (Figure 4.1). As long as these factors continue, the stock is said to be controlled by good quality and increasing demand. As a result, the rally should continue and there is no indication that it is near completion. Thus, action on the short side should be postponed, even if the stock appears to be an especially good short candidate.

No matter how strong a rally is, the demand that fuels it cannot be unlimited. At some point, the factors mentioned above will deteriorate, and as this occurs, the rally's completion draws closer. Instead of wider price spreads and increasing net upside progress from day to day, price spreads narrow and less progress is made. At this point, one of two things is happening: The stock is either meeting supply, which is trying to assume control, or the stock's demand is diminishing.

Knowing which process is underway is important. A determination can be made from the volume; increasing volume combined with narrower price spreads and less net upside progress as a rally progresses indicates that demand is being met by supply (Figure 4.2). Decreasing volume combined with narrower spreads and less progress, on the other hand, signals that demand is diminishing (Figure 4.3). Both provide warnings that the rally is nearly completed. Therefore, action on the short side may be considered. As a rule, ample supply should be considered to be a more negative indication than diminishing demand. If a rally is being stopped by supply being met, that means that supply is actually taking control of the stock away from demand, which is likely to result in a bigger decline after the rally has been completed. If a rally is being stopped by a withdrawal of demand, however, then supply is not automatically in control; the buyers in question are simply saying that at progressively higher prices they are progressively less willing to participate at this time. The buyers may return to the market when prices are somewhat lower, or their willingness to pay the current price may increase if the stock holds its gains following a withdrawal of demand.

FIGURE 4.1

Simulated stock and volume chart (Demand)

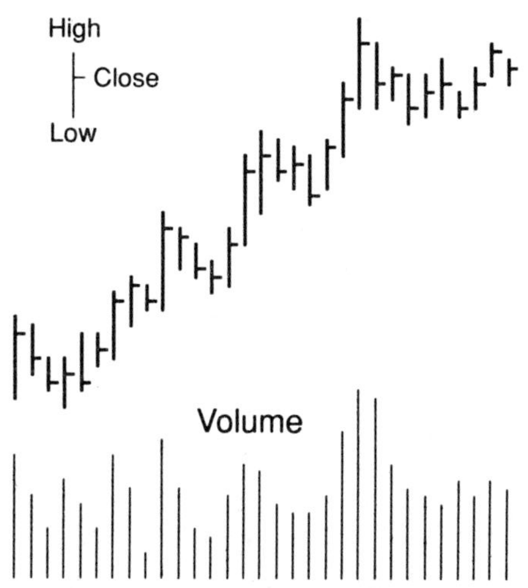

During an advance, good quality or increasing demand will tend to keep the rally going. The price range for the day will be large and the close will be the high for the day. The volume is greater on up days than the days where the market traded down.

THE IMPORTANCE OF JUDGMENT

Unfortunately, no single set of price spread, net progress and volume can be used to indicate a rally's completion. Judgment becomes very important at this point. For example, if two stocks have both been identified as potential short candidates and both appear to be equally weak to the market with the same proportion of downside potential, good judgment dictates the selection of the one that is meeting supply at the top of a rally rather than the one that is completing its rally because demand is diminishing. In this example, judgment is relatively limited due to all factors but one being the same. In the real world, opportunities are less likely to develop in such a clear-cut manner.

FIGURE 4.2

Simulated stock and volume chart (Supply)

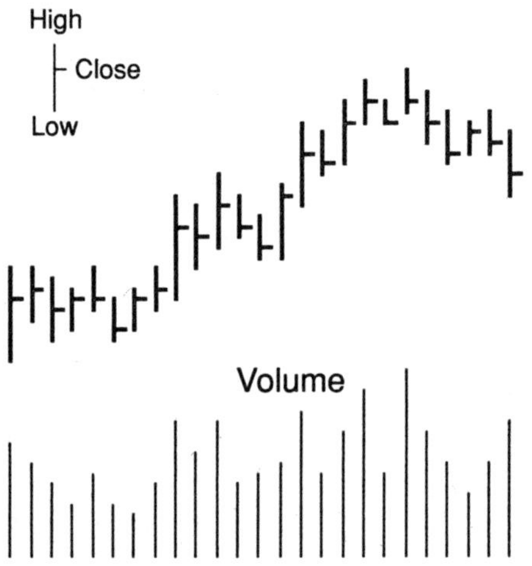

Witnessing the daily trading ranges becoming smaller with increasing volume during an advance indicates that demand is being met by supply. Signs of increasing supply is a negative indication.

Among the stocks that are meeting supply, some may be stopped immediately, while others continue to rally for several days until supply finally overwhelms demand. Judging each stock's relative weakness and downside potential may result in selecting an issue for a short position that continues to rally for several days after the position is established. The rally's continuation does not necessarily indicate poor judgment as long as the potential is sufficient to allow the proper placing of a stop order, allowing some continued upside progress.

Just as the action on a rally can indicate its completion and an opportunity on the short side, it can also signal the completion of a reaction. Supply controls a reaction. Increasing supply is reflected by widening price spread to the downside, increasing amounts of net downside progress and increasing volume. Like demand, supply is not unlimited; at some point, that supply will be withdrawn (Figure 4.4), or demand will overwhelm it. When the daily action indicates that one of these two processes is underway, it is time to seriously consider action on the long side.

FIGURE 4.3

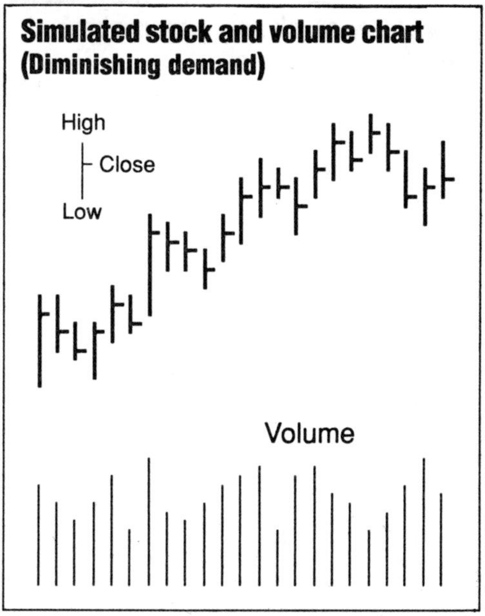

A sign of diminishing demand is decreasing volume and narrowing daily price ranges during an advance.

Not every change of character in the action should be viewed as a potential trading opportunity, however. This is where the current position in relation to previous action becomes important. For example, consider a stock that is in a previously defined uptrend. The stock is strong relative to the market and has a high enough objective to still be considered a candidate for a long position. The fact that the stock is in a well-defined uptrend indicates a readiness to move. However, this is not the readiness to move that is addressed in Step 4 of the Wyckoff method.

As a stock advances in an uptrend, it is normal for it to correct each small phase of the advance as it goes. At some point, it is normal to see the entire advance corrected. For the trader, the correction of each small phase of the advance is an opportunity on the long side. Wyckoff states that it is normal for a stock to correct to the vicinity of the halfway point of the move being corrected; this can be anywhere from a third to a two-thirds correction. When this zone is reached, begin watching the price and volume action more closely. Look for signs of demand being met or supply being withdrawn. Such action here calls for the consideration of new action on the long side.

FIGURE 4.4

Simulated stock and volume chart (Diminishing volume)

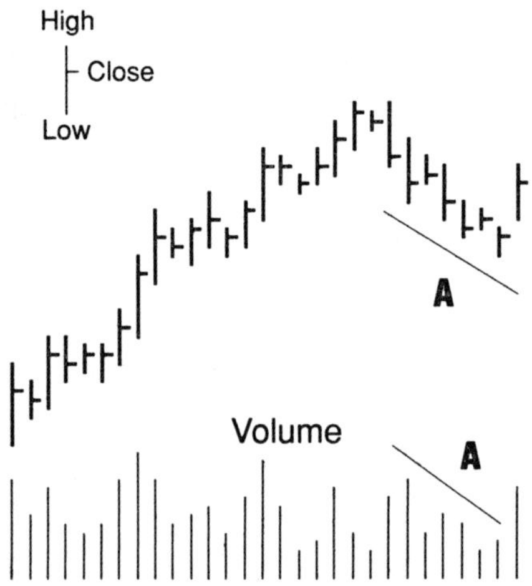

The declining prices along with diminishing volume indicate that supply is being withdrawn. A rally typically follows this situation.

Studying the Halfway Point

The longer-term investor can also use this concept of establishing positions near the halfway point. In this case, however, a broader perspective is necessary. Instead of trying to enter a position on the corrections of a minor phase of an extended advance, the investor should look for the correction of the entire advance to that point. When the correction is near the halfway point, it is time to start monitoring the price and volume action more closely. Again, the object is to identify either supply being met or demand being withdrawn. Note that this process is now being viewed on a broader scale; here it is likely that the indication given will not come from just two or three days' worth of action and more likely to be spread over a week or longer. Deciding whether to act comes from judging the character of the action as a whole near the halfway point. Although this example refers only to the long side, a similar but opposite set of considerations must be addressed for the short side.

The student of the Wyckoff method who chooses to limit him- or herself to stocks that are ready to move and that are already in defined up- or downtrends will do very well over time. However, this individual will need more than a little patience. Normally, stock action will spend more time in trading ranges than in either uptrends or downtrends. Thus, waiting for the completion of normal trend corrections is going to result in extended periods between trading opportunities. There is nothing wrong with waiting; however, for those who wish to expand their profit potential and increase the number of trading opportunities, there is the trading range action. Readiness to move with respect to trading range action can be divided into two categories: There is action that indicates a readiness to move from the bottom of a trading range to the top or from the top to the bottom, and there is also action that indicates a readiness to leave the trading range altogether and begin trending.

EXTENDED TRADING RANGE ACTION

For many investors and speculators, extended trading range action is the most frustrating of all. The common error is to view every rally as a likely breakout to the upside and every reaction as a breakout to the downside. From a profit standpoint, the result is a constant give-and-take, with the market doing both the giving and the taking. Frequently, the investor ends up with very little profit, or in worst cases less capital than when he started. Two preliminary steps can help avoid this: One is to avoid initiating any new action in the middle of a trading range, and the second is to approach every rally or reaction within a trading range with the idea that is going to be confined by the limits of the trading range.

The wisdom of avoiding new positions in the middle of a trading range should be obvious, but many fall victim to this error in their desire to remain active in the market. A trading range is a limited amount of vertical space; therefore, taking a position in the middle of the range automatically cuts the potential profit in half unless the selected reaction or rally is the one that leads to the breakout. This particular rule on avoiding the middle of the trading range becomes easier to apply if the area to avoid is specifically outlined. One way to do so is to divide the trading range vertically into thirds, with the middle third the one to avoid. Another approach is to divide the range into quarters and avoid the middle two. This approach will result in fewer trading opportunities, but those that do develop should have greater profit potential.

Consider next the stock that is in a trading range exactly six points wide. The point and a half just above the bottom of the trading range is the area in which to consider long positions. The one and a half points of the top of the trading range is the area in which to consider short positions. It is reasonable to expect the stock to rally from the lower quarter to the upper quarter of the range and to react from the upper quarter to the lower quarter. Therefore, a move of four and a half points may be anticipated. The use of a 3-to-1 profit/risk ratio in this case calls for a stop order placed one and a half points above or below the entry price. If the stock is in the upper or lower quarter of the range when the position is established, the stop will be outside the limits of the range, making it less vulnerable to being triggered except where the stock is actually leaving the range. In such cases, being stopped out should be welcome, especially if the investor has been able to ride the stock up and down several times within the range.

Trading range action is such that many stocks will at some point penetrate the support or resistance level of a trading range without achieving a breakout. For the range trader, these instances can be especially frustrating, since the likelihood of being stopped out is good just before a move in the anticipated direction begins. Frequently, these penetrations of support and resistance that do not lead to immediate breakouts are followed by price movement in the opposite direction. Wyckoff refers to these as spring and upthrust actions.

Some stocks move independently of the general market. Most, however, move with it. This is what makes a fifth and final step to the Wyckoff method necessary. The investor who chooses to act only on the basis of the first four steps takes a greater risk than is necessary; he risks trading against the market, which usually results in a loss. In addition, the risk of being premature is greater, frequently resulting in being stopped out just before the anticipated move gets underway. The fifth step, which I will consider in the next chapter, tells the investor to time positions in individual stocks to anticipated turns in the general market.

5
Timing Your Commitments

The Wyckoff method ends where it begins — with the general market. Step 5 of the Wyckoff method, the final step and the topic of this chapter's discussion of the Wyckoff method, instructs the Wyckoff student to time positions in individual issues to anticipated turns in the general market.

The logic of this is easy to understand. If the first four steps of the Wyckoff method have been correctly applied, the results will be enhanced by a market that is moving with a particular position. While it is true that all markets will have issues that make substantial moves counter to the prevailing trend, most individual stocks will go with the trend following the line of least resistance. The odds of achieving success are improved by selecting positions from the majority rather than from trying to identify the minority.

To review, Richard Wyckoff stated the basics of his course in stock market science and technique in five steps:

Step 1: Determine the present position and probable future trend of the market. Then decide how you are going to play the game: long, short or neutral.

Step 2: Select from those stocks in harmony with the market the ones stronger than the market in a bull market. In a bear market, select those that are weaker than the market.

Step 3: Select those stocks that have built up a cause, a potential count for a move in keeping with your goals.

Step 4: Determine each stock's readiness to move. Analyze the vertical and figure charts of the candidates with the help of buying and selling tests.

Step 5: Time your commitments with a turn in the market.

By employing all five steps, the investor or speculator can determine what type of market operation to undertake, which individual stocks or bonds represent the best candidate(s) and when the best time is to make a commitment.

Gauging the Trend

Step 5 tells us the best time to make a commitment in individual issues is the point at which we can anticipate a turn in the general market. Anticipating a turn in the general market requires the use of a general market index. Indices come in a variety of shapes and sizes. Some are very broadly defined, using the action of most of the individual issues. Others, like the Wyckoff wave, are very narrowly defined by the action of just a few key issues. Though no one index is perfect, all the indices in their own way reflect market action. Therefore, the individual investor need not agonize over the selection of an index. However, once the selection is made, it is best to remain faithful to that index; hopping from index to index can be dangerous because it allows the investor to seek out the index that most closely confirms a preconceived conclusion rather than using the index to arrive at the conclusion.

Learning to anticipate a turn in the general market requires an understanding of all three of the basic laws of the Wyckoff method: supply and demand, cause and effect, and effort vs. result. Supply and demand are represented in the action of a general market index just as they are represented in individual stocks. A turn in the general market will occur when either demand or supply is sufficiently met to overwhelm the other, or when demand or supply is sufficiently withdrawn to leave the other in control. As outlined in step 4 of the Wyckoff method, the meeting of or withdrawal of supply or demand can be seen in a vertical line chart of the index's action.

As a review of this extremely important concept, consider the chart of the weekly Wyckoff wave in Figure 5.1. The move from point A to point B illustrates some aspects of supply and demand. Note that during the six weeks from A to B, the weekly price spreads remained wide except during the final week. Volume increased through week 4 (point X). It then contracted somewhat on week 5 and contracted substantially on week 6. From A to X, the advance was very healthy; increasing volume was producing consistently wide price spreads and good net progress. This combination indicates increasing demand.

Week 5, which immediately follows point X, shows a change of character. Price spread is again relatively wide, but volume is reduced. Something has changed. One possible explanation is that demand is being withdrawn due to the higher prices. This reduces the buyers' control and gives supply more control. Another possible explanation is that during the week, supply came in and overwhelmed demand, accounting for the poorest close to that point. Either way, the change of character tells the investor looking for an opportunity on the short side to pay closer attention.

During week 6 (point B), the market attempts to extend its advance. The sharp drop in volume indicates a decisive withdrawal of demand, and a turn in the general market may be anticipated. The investor may now reexamine the stocks he previously identified in steps 1 through 4 of the Wyckoff method as being good short candidates and may consider establishing a short position if the criteria required by the first four steps are still being met. It is not necessary that the general market immediately turn down to qualify as a market turn. Since the anticipation of a turn is justified, and taking into account that some stocks or stock groups fall in and out of favor, those stocks that Steps 1 through 4 revealed to be

FIGURE 5.1, part a

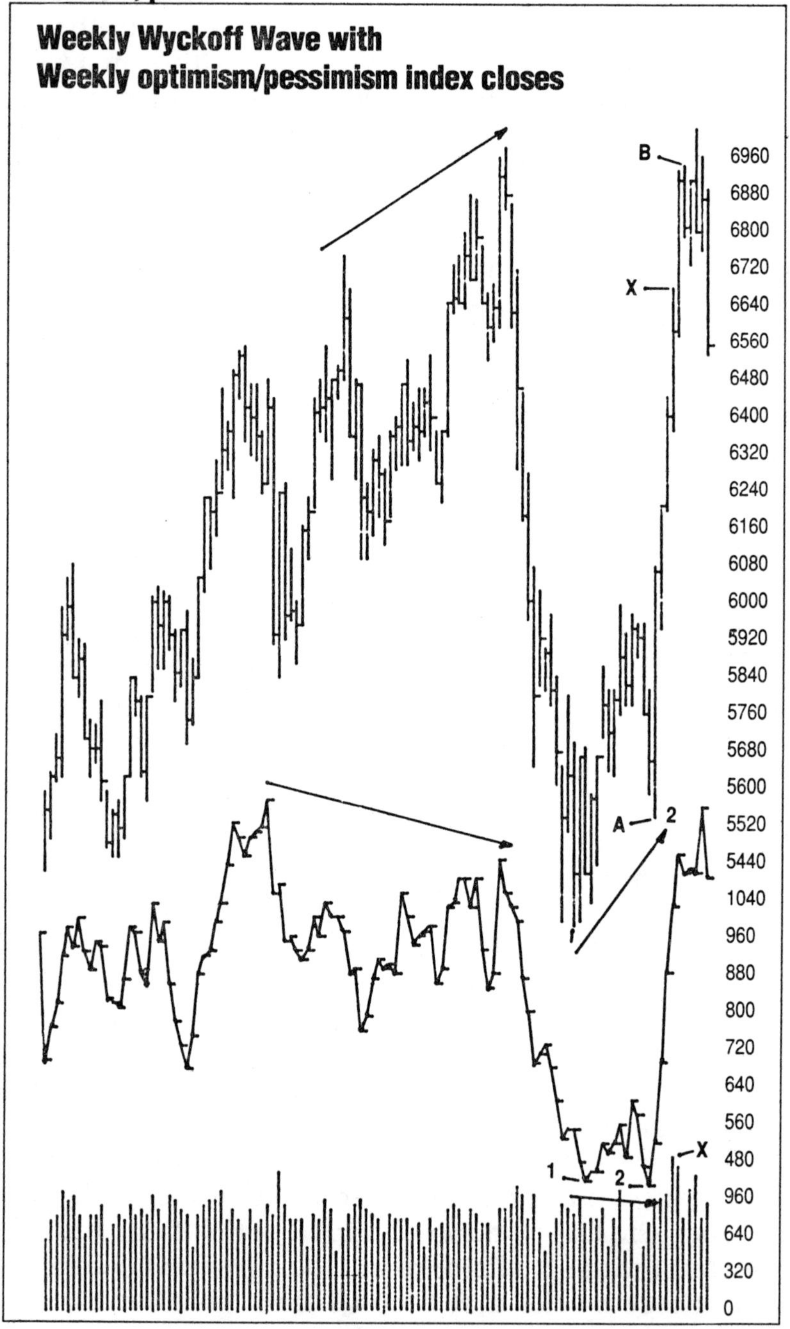

good short candidates should be some of the first to turn down.

CAUSE AND EFFECT

The law of cause and effect is also important in anticipating a turn. Examining the supply and demand factors in Figure 5.1 revealed a problem with the character of the advance, suggesting the possibility of a turn. However, a cause as indicated by a figure chart is required to convert that possibility to a reality. Consider the 10-point modified figure chart of the Wyckoff wave in Figure 5.2 as it appeared at the close of week 6 (point B). The horizontal build-up of postings between the 6750 level and the 6900 level represents potential, or a cause.

Since a turn is anticipated, we measure the cause as a

FIGURE 5.1, part b

Price and volume

For the period from A to B (January 14 through February 22):

	Price spread	Volume
Week 1 (A)	527.5 points.	916,260,000 shares
Week 2	264.0	901,460,000
Week 3	238.875	973,060,000
Week 4 (X)	296.75	1,299,590,000
Week 5	347.25	1,195,590,000
Week 6 (B)	152.375	776,930,000

Average for weeks 1 through 5:

Price spread: 334.875 points
Volume: 1.057,192 shares

Figure 5.1, parts a and b

The optimism/pessimism index moved to a new low (point 2) while the Wyckoff wave did not. The new low by the optimism/pessimism index indicated heavy volume (a measure of effort). The Wyckoff wave held above the previous low (a measure of result). Effort versus result were not in harmony. This divergence indicated a change in the market. During the weeks from point A to B, the price spread remained wide, indicating strong demand.

downside potential, or count. The result is the anticipated downside objective following the anticipated turn. The count is measured at the top of the areas that represent the cause to keep the indicated objective as conservative as possible. This particular potential has two phases. Phase A is the more conservative. It indicates a potential decline of 160 points from the count level to 6740. The mechanics of this projection are as follows: the distance from the right side of phase A to the left side includes 16 horizontal divisions on the figure chart. Since this is a 10-point modified figure chart where each vertical division represents a 10-point move, the 16 horizontal divisions are multiplied by the number of points represented by each vertical division. The result is 160 points.

Phase B represents a more aggressive downside potential. It is measured from the point where phase A ends to the left side of the potential. This area covers an additional 16 horizontal divisions, indicating an additional 160 points of potential. The potential indicated by phase B is added to that indicated by phase A. The result is 320 points for an objective of 6580, which represents a move of approximately 4.5%. A 4.5% move may not seem worthwhile, but it should be remembered that a 4.5% potential move does not mean that every stock is going to decline 4.5%. Some will not decline at all. Some will continue to move higher, and some will outperform the market to the downside. Some of these stocks should be already represented in the group of short candidates previously identified by Steps 1 through 4. As a general rule, never establish a position in a stock that has less potential than the general market.

EFFORT VS. RESULT

The law of effort vs. result is a third important factor in anticipating a turn in the general market. Effort and result should move in harmony. When they do not, a turn in the market is suggested. Result is measured by price movement, which is reflected in the Wyckoff wave. Effort is measured by the flow of volume, which is reflected in the optimism/pessimism (OP) index (see the sidebar entitled "The optimism/pessimism index"). Each trading day is made up of buying

FIGURE 5.2

10-point modified Wyckoff wave figure chart

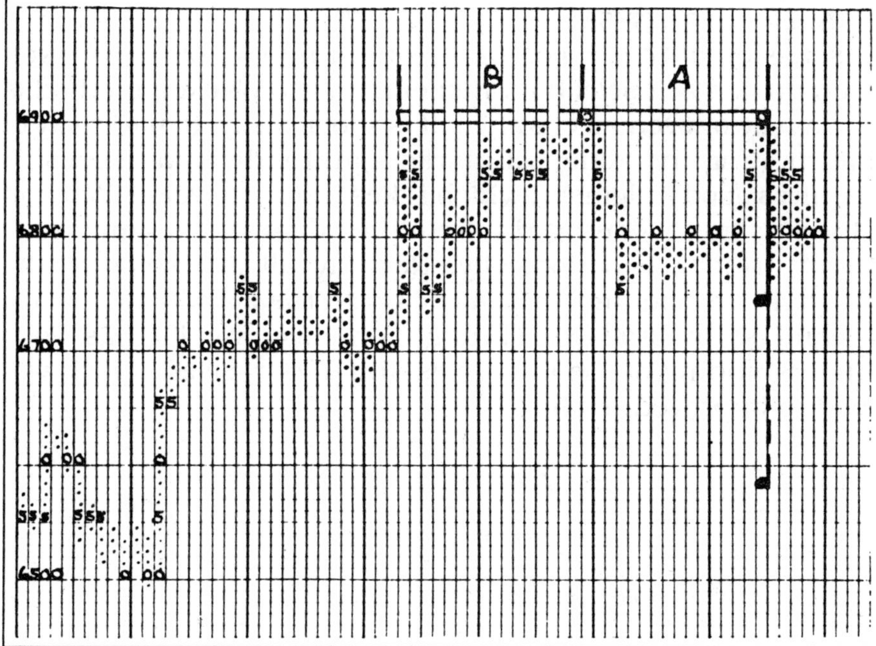

Price objectives are determined by measuring the horizontal count on the figure chart and projecting down from the upper boundary.

waves and selling waves. The trading volume during buying waves is added to the OP index. Trading volume during selling waves is subtracted from the index. The net effect is posted as a continuous line. On the weekly chart of the Wyckoff wave, the OP index is posted between the volume and the wave (Figure 5.1).

Compare points 1 and 2 as marked on the Wyckoff wave to similar points marked on the OP index. Note that while point 2 on the OP index is lower than point 1, point 2 on the Wyckoff wave is higher than point 1. Effort and result are not in harmony. From point 1 to point 2, there was too much downside effort for the result, indicating the likelihood of a change in direction for the Wyckoff wave. The investor seeking to identify potential long candidates should use this anticipated turn as justification for considering long positions.

PRACTICE, PRACTICE

Discussion of Step 5 completes our summary of the Wyckoff method of stock selection. Remember, the Wyckoff method is not magic or even mechanical. It is a logical, systematic way of interpreting the action of markets and individual issues. It requires good judgment, which takes time to develop. Wyckoff students are encouraged to reinforce their understanding of these principles periodically. Restudy all five steps of the Wyckoff method and then move on to the equally important second step: *practice*. Through practice, we increase our understanding of the principles and of ourselves, which will lead to improved results.

Glossary

Accumulate a line—Add to a previous market position.

Accumulation—Another term for buying; an accumulation area is a sideways price movement implying buyers are willing to purchase at current prices.

Bear—One who expects a decline in market prices (short).

Bull—One who expects a rise in market prices (long).

Composite average—Composite broad-based average examples are Standard & Poor's (S&P) 500, Value Line, Wilshire 5000.

Congestion Area or Pattern—A series of trading days in which there is no visible progress in price.

Consolidation—Also known as a congestion period. A pause that allows participants in a market to reevaluate the market and sets the stage for the next price move.

Correction—Any price reaction within the market leading to an adjustment by as much as one-third to two-thirds of the previous gain.

Cover—Offsetting or neutralizing a prior transaction, such as buying an equivalent number of shares and delivering against a short position.

Cover—Purchasing back a contract sold earlier.

Danger point—A price one to five points under a support level, above a resistance level, above or below a 50% reaction or rally mark, or under a clearly defined support or supply line.

Distribution—Another term for selling large blocks of stock; a distribution area is a narrow price range over a long period of time, implying sellers are disappointed but buyers are willing to purchase.

Group average—Includes such entities as the Dow Jones 30 Industrials "30 stocks," Transportation Index, and Utilities. Group averages are often grouped by industry, such as aerospace, steel, airlines.

GTC—Good till canceled, the usual status of a stop order.

Issue—A class ownership such as a common stock, bond, option or contract.

Leading—A stock or average whose price reacts up or down before most other stocks.

Long—Acquisition of an investment instrument such as a security, futures contract or option (as call).

Markdown—A day-by-day price range decrease.

Markup—A day-by-day price range increase.

Odd lot—Less than 100 shares of a particular stock.

Office stop, buy stop—Instructions to a broker to begin a long or short transaction when a stock's market price reaches a certain level.

Overbought/oversold—The general expressed opinion is that the price of the market has overreached itself, thus requiring a sideways movement, price retracement, or consolidation.

Overbought—Too rapid acceleration of rally or advance; lack or corrective reactions or resting spells during an advance. Price is sensitive to sales and withdrawal of experienced buyers.

Oversold position—When liquidation is temporarily or permanently finished. It usually occurs at the end of a big decline or the last stages of a decline—all those who could be induced to sell have done so; stocks are in the hands of experienced operators. Sellers are weak and buyers are strong.and able to carry what they have bought through any further declines; amateur shorts still hanging in at the end of decline are a bullish factor because they have to buy back (cover) what they sold short.

Oversold—Too rapid reaction, or decline. Price becomes highly sensitive to short covering and withdrawal of experienced sellers. Lack of corrective rallies or resting spells during a downswing.

Point and figure chart—A price-only chart that takes into account only whole integer changes in price, i.e., a two-point change

Price—The amount of money for which an issue is bought or sold.

Reaction normally half a rise—Not a must, just a reference point for technical strength or weakness (less than half is strong, more than half is weak).

Resistance—The historical price at which sellers tend to sell a particular stock; also the historical price that usually indicates a coming decline in the price of a particular stock.

Rotation—Moving funds from one sector to another sector of the stock market as the business cycle unfolds.

Round lot—100 shares of a particular stock.

Shake-out—A period of increased volume after a price move attributed to weak, unsure hands unloading their holdings.

Short—Sale of an investment instrument not yet owned in the hope of making covering purchase later at a lower price, thereby making a profit.

Spring—Another term for upthrust; occurs when price moves above a pivot top and a widespread reversal ensues as follows: a) two previous closes are reversed, b) close is below pivot top, c) close is below opening and mid-range, d) daily price range is greater than the previous day's range.

Springboard—The point in a stock's movement when it is ready for a plunge or a rise. In a bull move, this is usually at the bottom of a decline; in a bear move, it occurs at the top of an advance.The beginning of a springboard is at the bottom of the range of accumulation or an upper level of that range of distribution (but not when it breaks the old line of resistance or support).

Stop loss order—Instructions to buy or sell an issue when its market price meets a specified loss.

Stop Loss—The risk management technique in which the trade is liquidated to halt any further decline in value.

Stop order—An instruction to a broker to sell long or buy short "at the market" when the price reaches a stipulated level. Buy stops are orders that are placed at a predetermined price over the current price of the market. The order becomes a "buy at the market" order if the market is at or above to the price of the stop order. Sell stops are orders that are placed with a predetermined price below the current price. Sell-stop orders become "sell at the market" orders if the market trades at or below the price of the stop order.

Supply and demand—Prices rise when buyer demand exceeds seller supply, and vice versa when supply and demand are balanced, price fluctuates in a range.

Support—A historical price level at which falling prices have stopped falling and either moved sideways or reversed direction; usually seen as a price chart pattern.

Swings—The measurement of movement of the price of a tradeable between extreme highs and lows.

Technical position—Refers to the ability of stock owners to hold onto their purchases. A stock is technically weak when it's held mainly by the public who can't or won't hold onto it. A stock is technically strong when held mainly by large-scale trader/investors who have the ability to ride out cyclical behavior.

Terminal shakeout—A rapid downward price movement occurring at or near the end of extensive preparation for an advance.

Thrust—A sharp price run up and out of an area of distribution, or a temporary bulge through the top of a trading range that does not hold and indicates weakness.

Trade—The act or process of buying and/or selling.

Trading Range—The difference between the high and low prices traded during a period of time.

Trendline—A line drawn that connects either a series of highs or lows in a trend. The trendline can represent either support as in an uptrend line or resistance as in a downtrend line. Consolidations are marked by horizontal trendlines.

Trend—The general drift, tendency, or bent of a set of statistical data as related to time.

Turning point—The time when a rising market (rally) or a declining market (reaction) has halted and is about to reverse.

Upthrust—Occurs when price moves above a pivot top and a wide-spread reversal ensues as follows: a) two previous closes are reversed, b) close is below pivot top, c) close is below opening and mid-range, d) daily price range is greater than the previous day's range.

Volume—The number of issues traded over a specific time period such as a day.

Wave chart—A vertical line chart (bar chart) of the price sum of the top few stocks of an industry group.

Zone of resistance—Opposite of *zone of support*.

Zone of support—Period of time during which market price and volume are indicating that the prevailing downward price motion has met substantial buying interest and may be preparing for a reversal.

List of Figures

Index

R

S

T